iPhone Application Sketch Book

■ ■ ■

Dean Kaplan

Apress®

iPhone Application Sketch Book

Copyright © 2009 by Kaplan Software Group, Inc.

ISBN-13 (pbk): 978-1-4302-2823-3

Editorial Board: Clay Andres, Steve Anglin, Mark Beckner, Ewan Buckingham, Tony Campbell, Gary Cornell, Jonathan Gennick, Michelle Lowman, Matthew Moodie, Jeffrey Pepper, Frank Pohlmann, Ben Renow-Clarke, Dominic Shakeshaft, Matt Wade, Tom Welsh
Compositor: Dean Kaplan

Distributed to the book trade worldwide by Springer-Verlag New York, Inc., 233 Spring Street, 6th Floor, New York, NY 10013. Phone 1-800-SPRINGER, fax 201-348-4505, e-mail **orders-ny@springer-sbm.com,** or visit **http://www.springeronline.com**.

For information on translations, please e-mail **info@apress.com**, or visit **http://www.apress.com**.

Apress and friends of ED books may be purchased in bulk for academic, corporate, or promotional use. eBook versions and licenses are also available for most titles. For more information, reference our Special Bulk Sales–eBook Licensing web page at **http://www.apress.com/info/bulksales**.

Introduction

The *iPhone Application Sketch Book* is the brainchild of Dean Kaplan, founder of Kapsoft (1996). A member of the "Made for iPod, Works with iPhone" program, Kapsoft is currently deeply involved in new and exciting accessory development for the iPhone platform. Dean understood the need for a simple and effective iPhone design tool that lead to the iPhone Application Sketch Book. Apress saw the simplicity and functionality of this tool and worked with Dean to publish this book to a wider audience.

This sketch book gives users 75 pages of grid space to draw and lay out their iPhone application ideas. The grid background helps users keep their designs organized, while the life-size iPhone template gives the designer a true idea of what the finished product will render.

The sketch book features

- A grid background on each page
- A lay-flat binding so that you can have one hand on the phone and one on a pencil
- Seventy-five pages to write, draw, compose, and doodle on
- An organized place for your user interface designs
- Perforations so that you can take the pages out if you wish

We hope that you will find this book useful for whatever purpose you choose.

About the Author

Dean Kaplan is founder and owner of Kapsoft, a technology consulting firm specializing in software applications for engineering applications. Kapsoft provides a full spectrum of product design and development services including manufacturing automation, cellular and location services, material handling, automatic identification, network analysis and protocols, telecommunications, telecom billing, healthcare, and bond trading. Dean recently designed and executed a new synthetic instrument product serving as a replacement for five or more legacy RF test instruments.

Dean anticipated a need for simple effective iPhone design tools and created the *iPhone Application Sketch Book* to fill that void. Kapsoft is a member of the "Made for iPod - Works with iPhone" program and is currently deeply involved in new exciting accessory development for the iPhone platform. More information about the *iPhone Application Sketch Book* and other related iPhone design products may be obtained at MobileSketchBook.com.

Dean Kaplan was born in Philadelphia and to this day still resides in nearby Haverford, Pennsylvania. Dean has a Bachelor of Science in Electrical Engineering Technology obtained from Temple University in 1982. Dean writes a contemporary technology blog at DeanOnSoftware.com. For info about Kapsoft, please see Kapsoft.com. You can also follow Dean on Twitter at @Kapsoft.

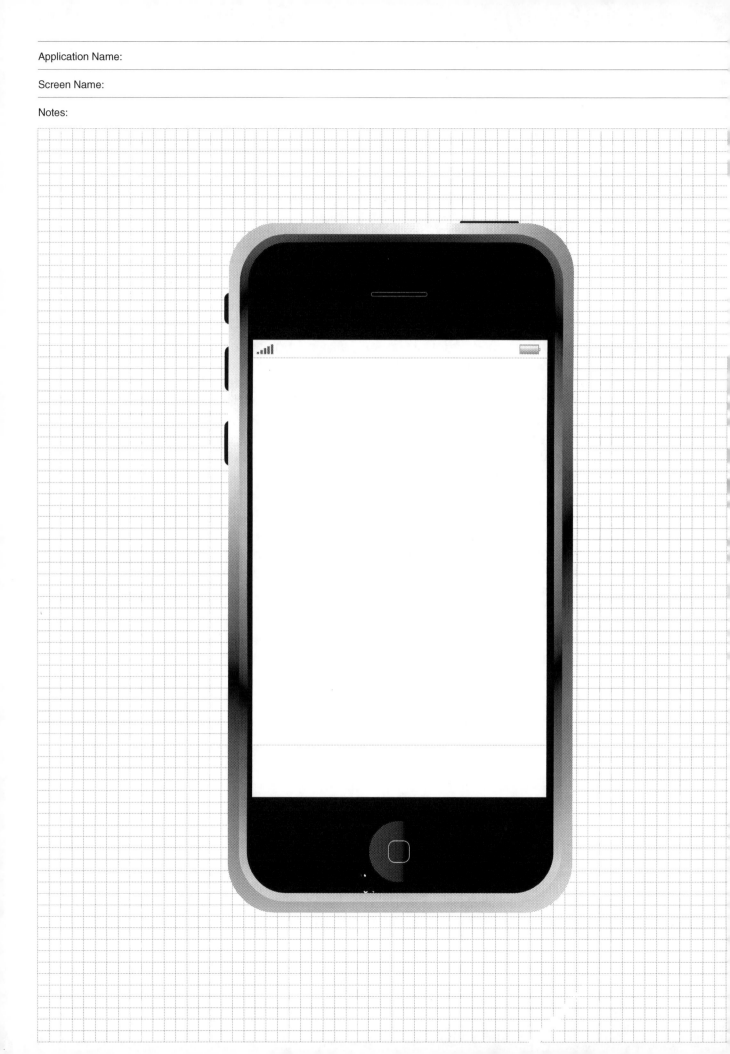

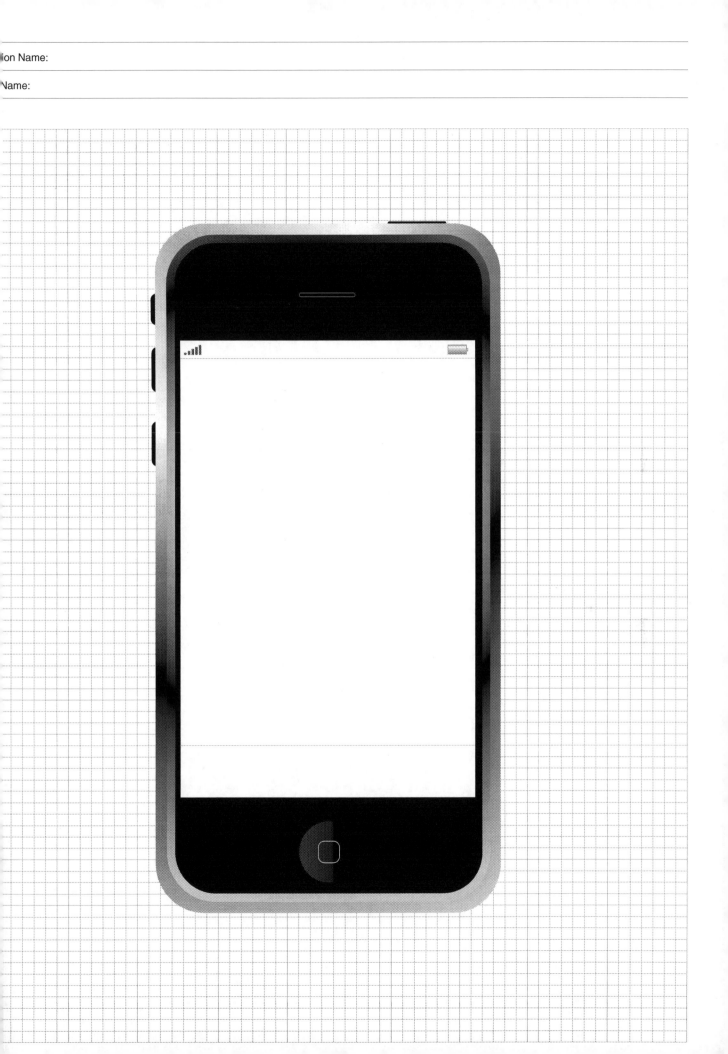

Application Name:

Screen Name:

Notes:

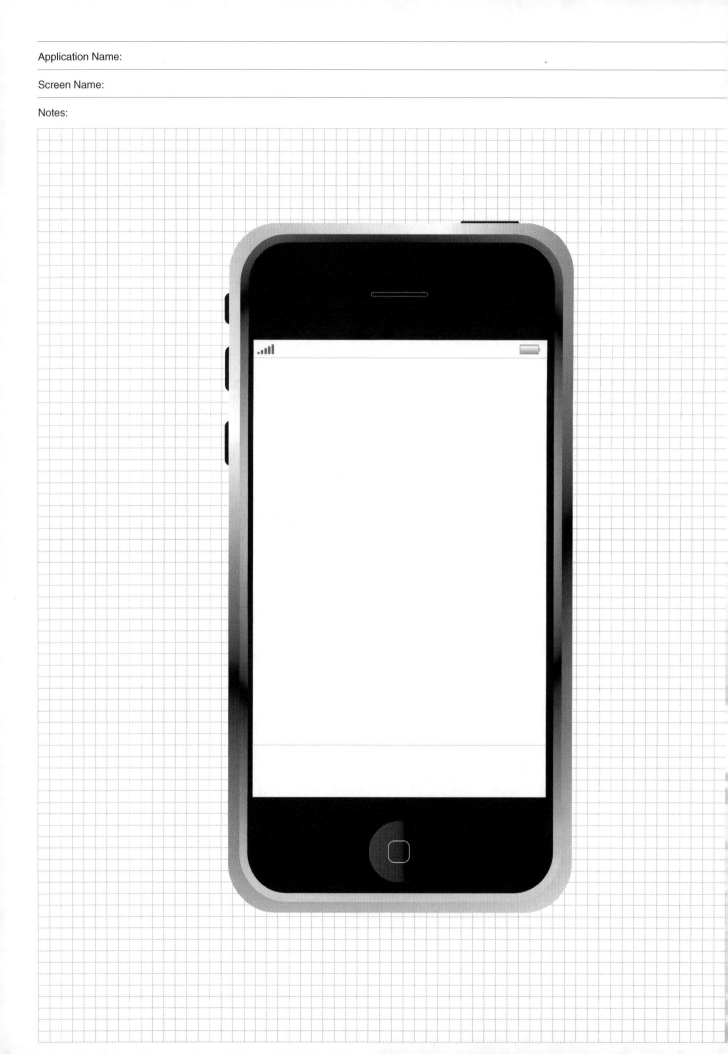

Application Name:

Screen Name:

Notes:

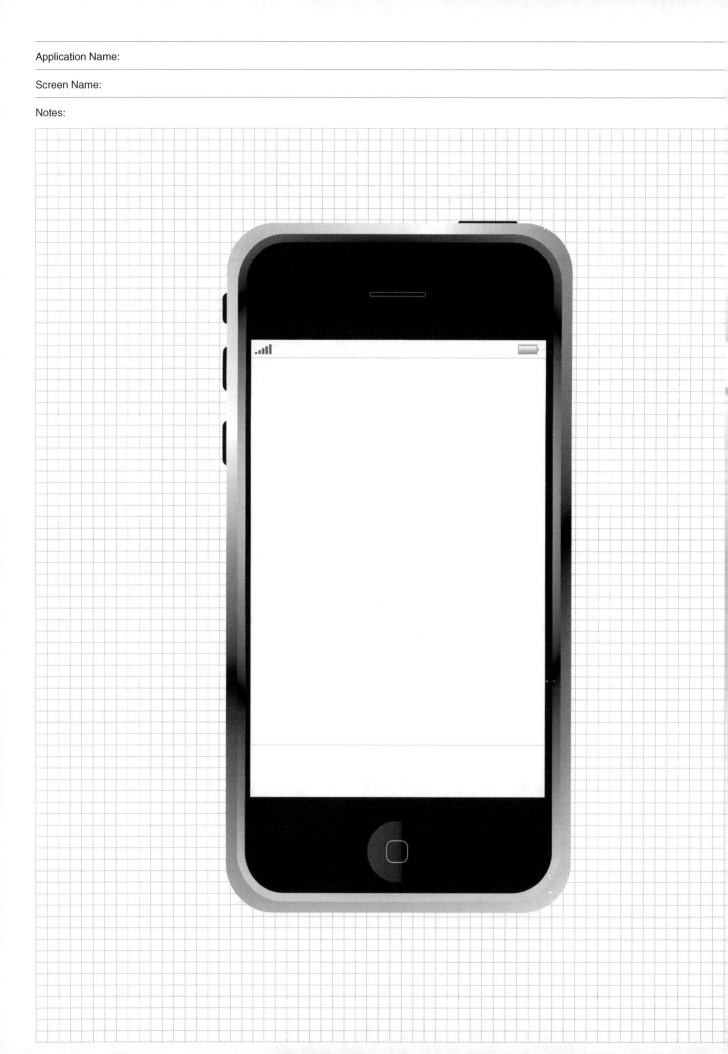

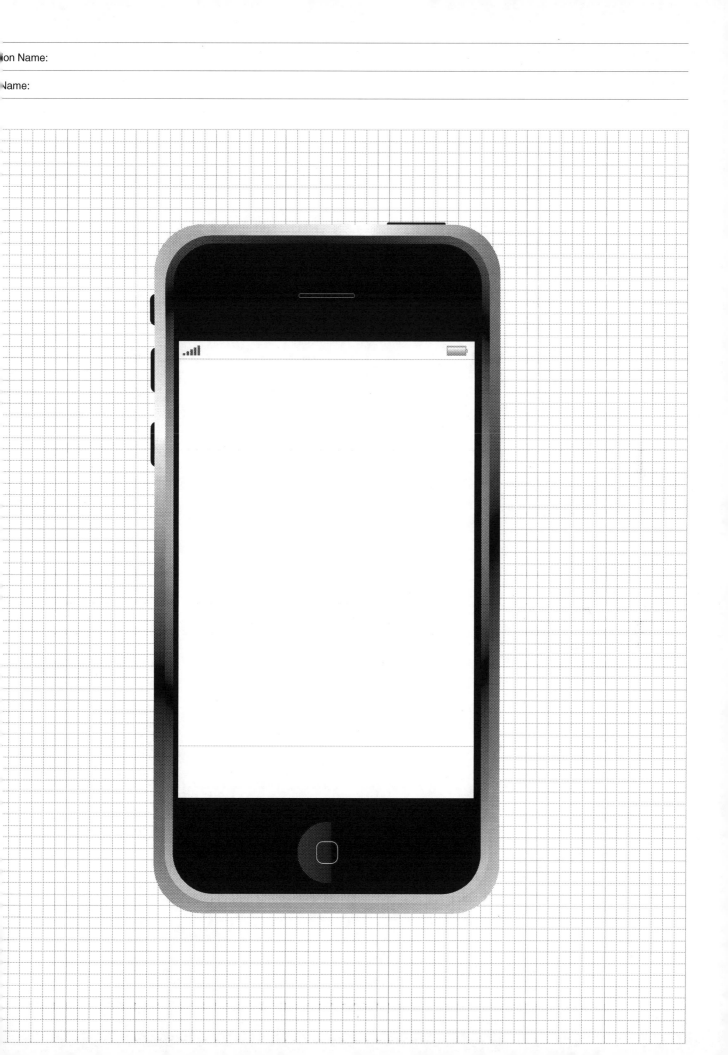

Application Name:

Screen Name:

Notes:

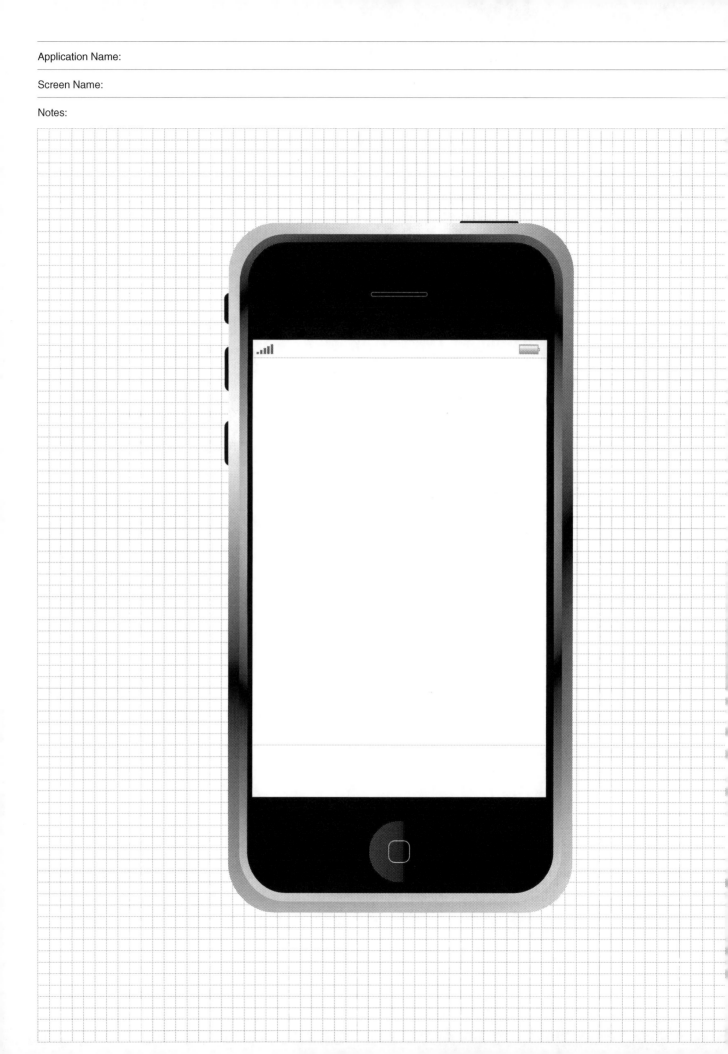

Application Name:

Screen Name:

Notes:

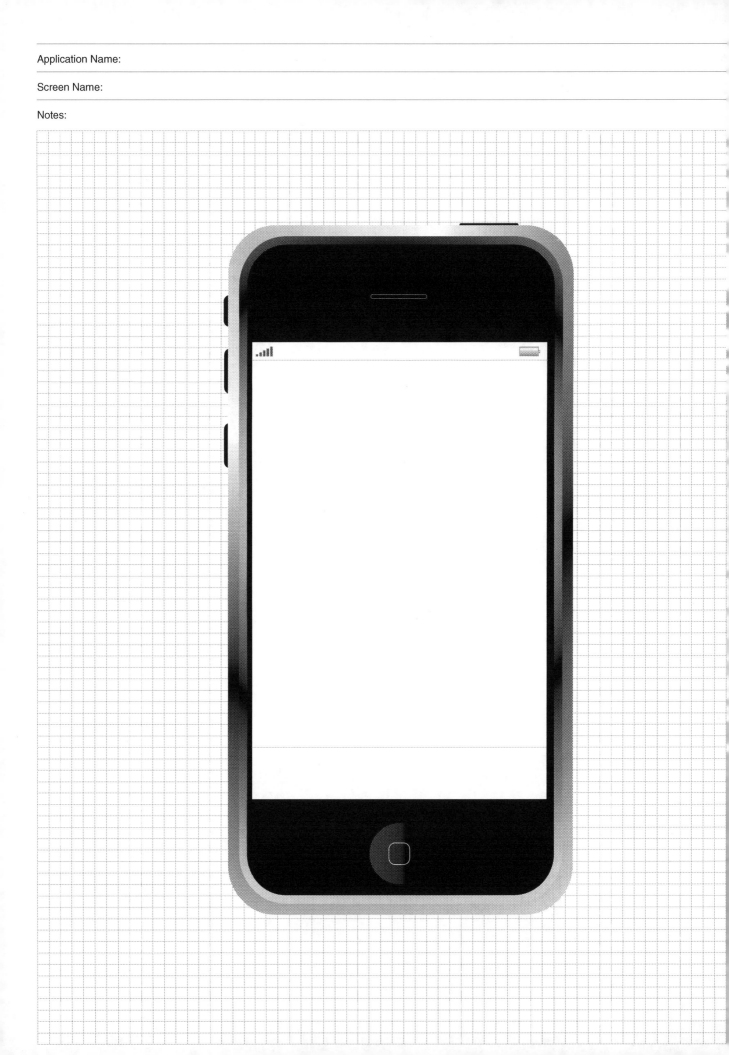

Application Name:

Screen Name:

Notes:

Application Name:

Screen Name:

Notes:

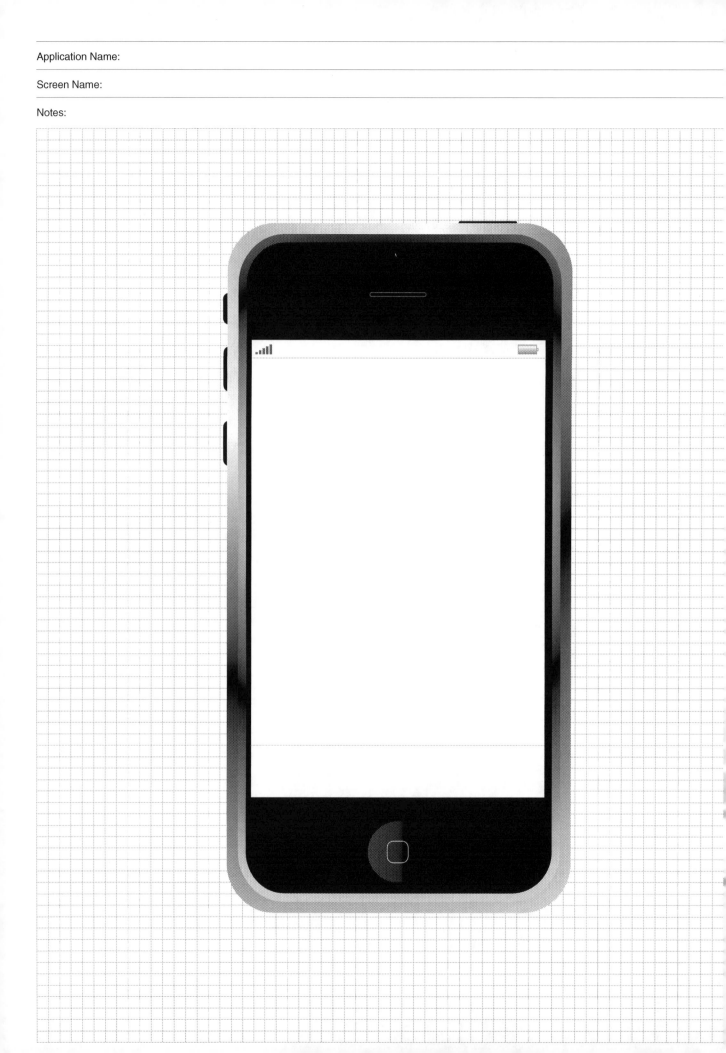

Application Name:

Screen Name:

Notes:

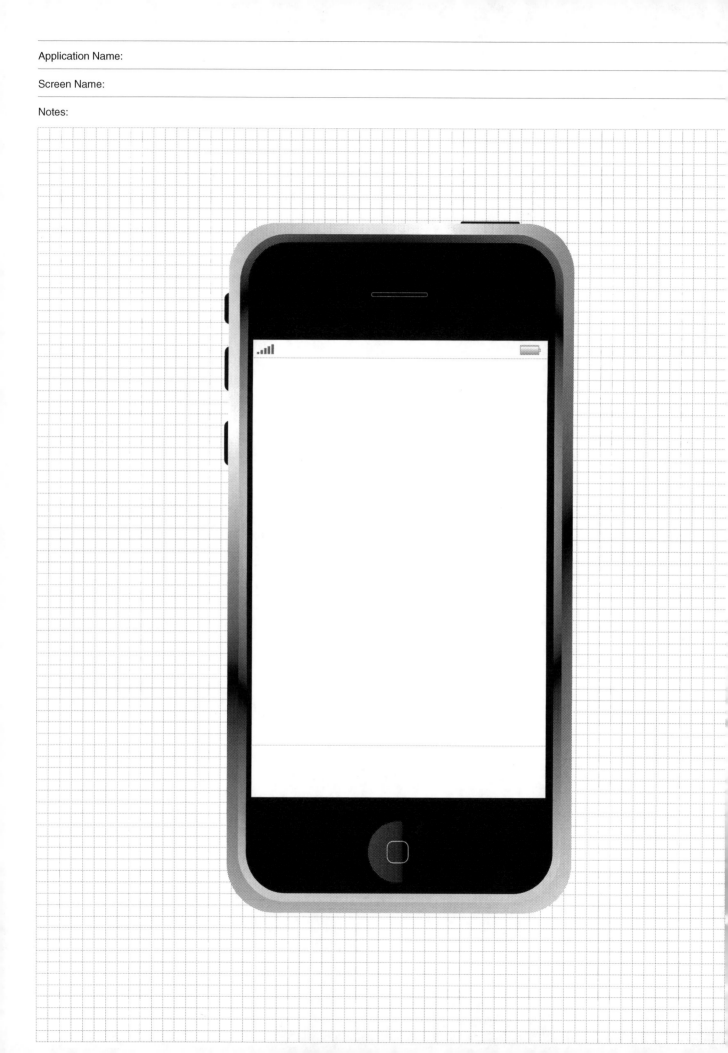

ion Name:

Name:

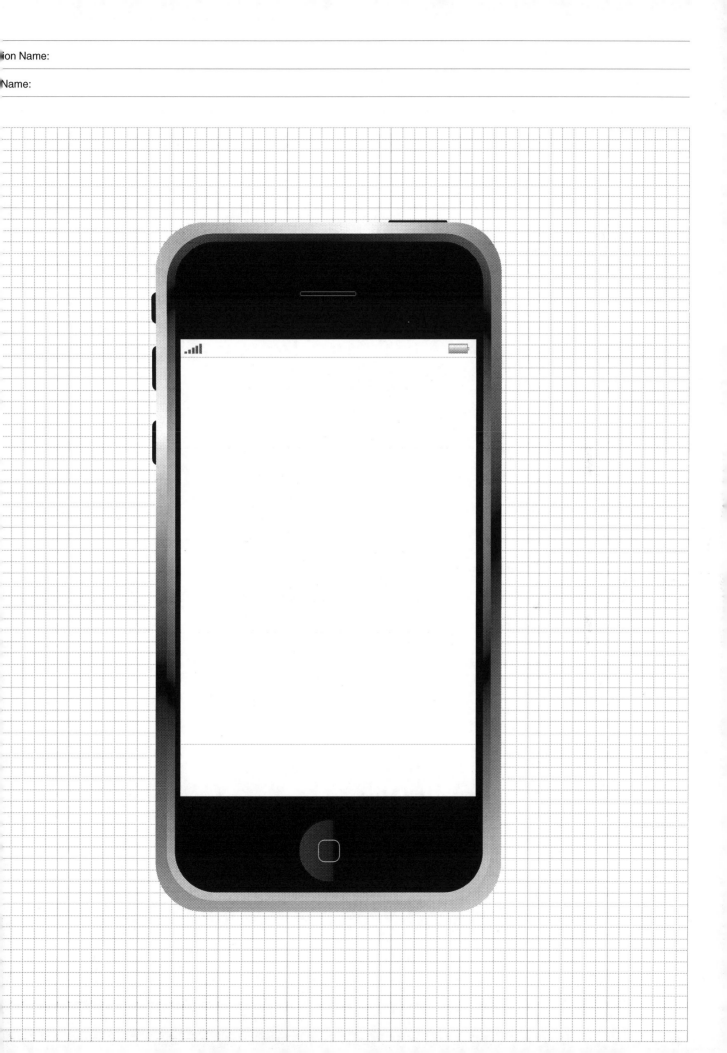

Application Name:

Screen Name:

Notes:

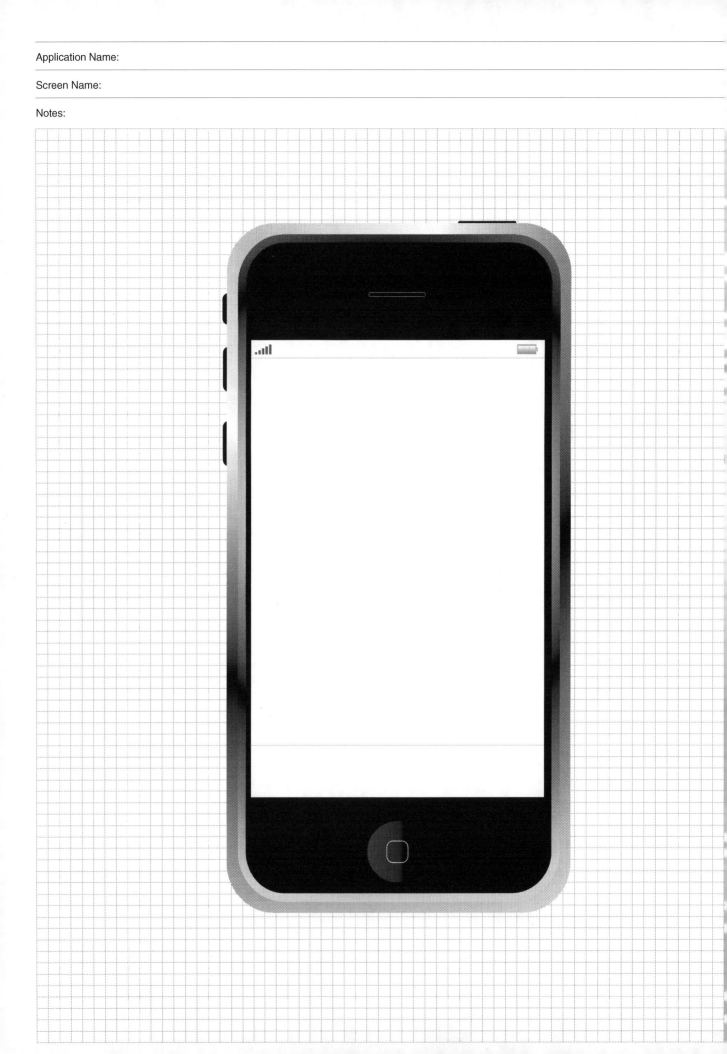

Application Name:

Screen Name:

Notes:

Application Name:

Screen Name:

Notes:

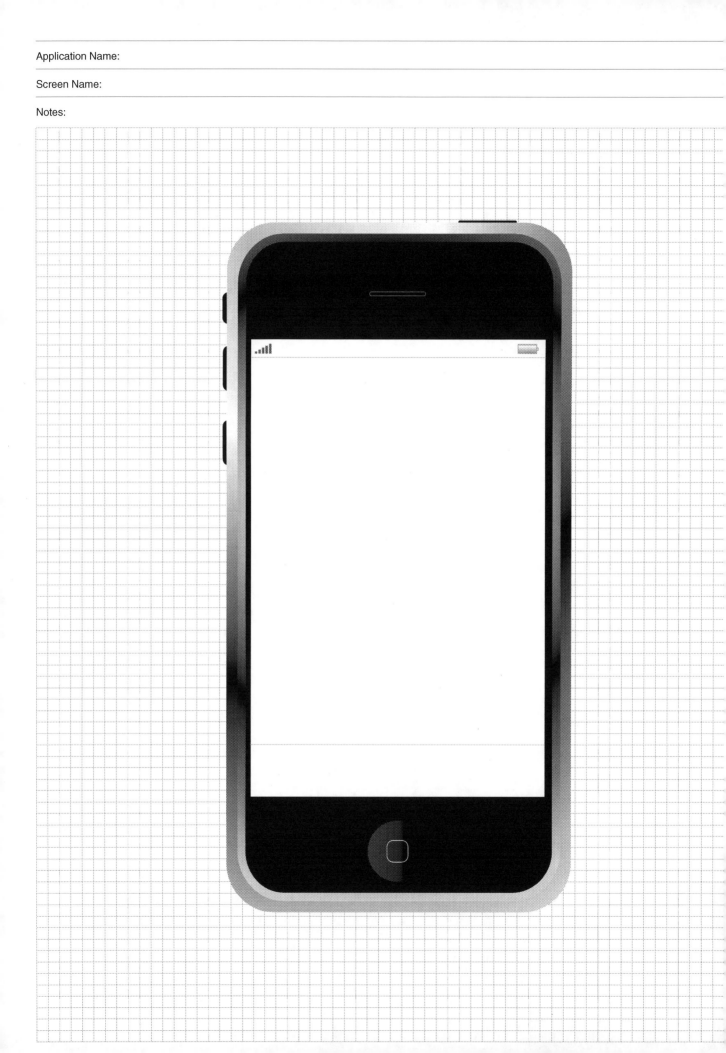

Application Name:

Screen Name:

Notes:

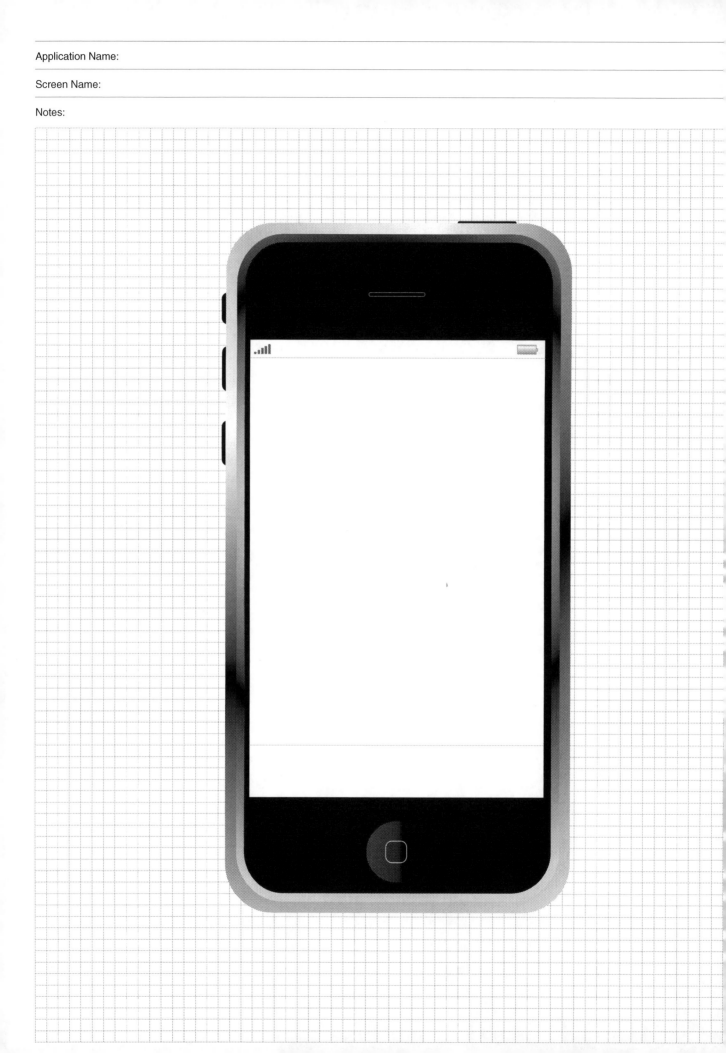

Application Name:

Screen Name:

Notes:

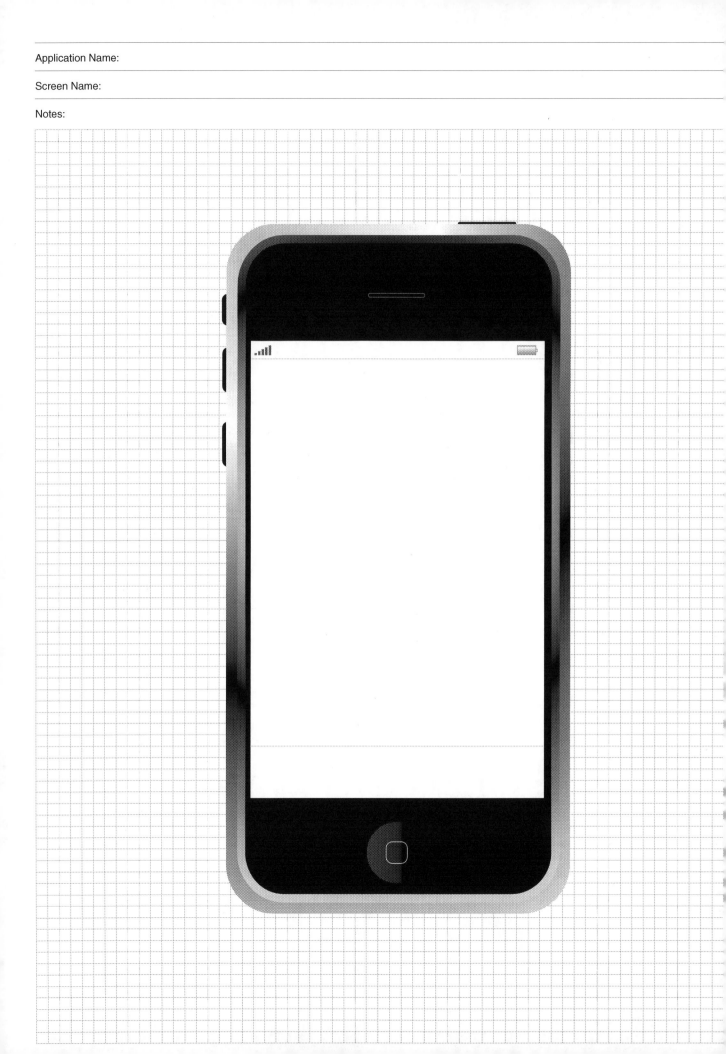

Application Name:

Screen Name:

Notes:

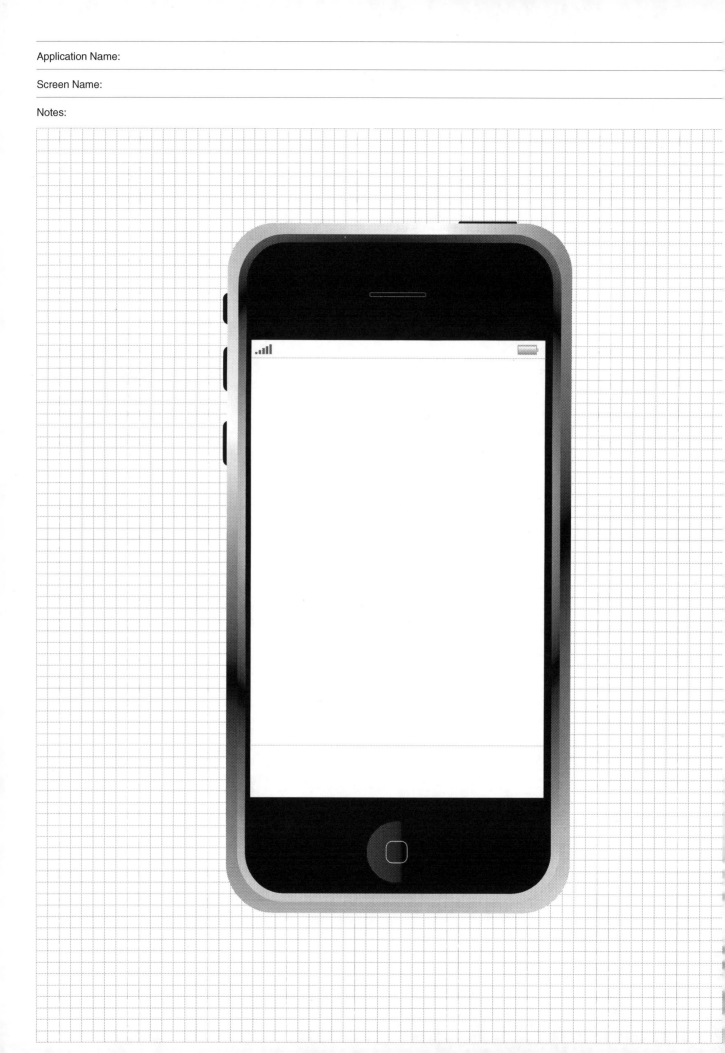

Application Name:

Screen Name:

Notes:

Application Name:

Screen Name:

Notes:

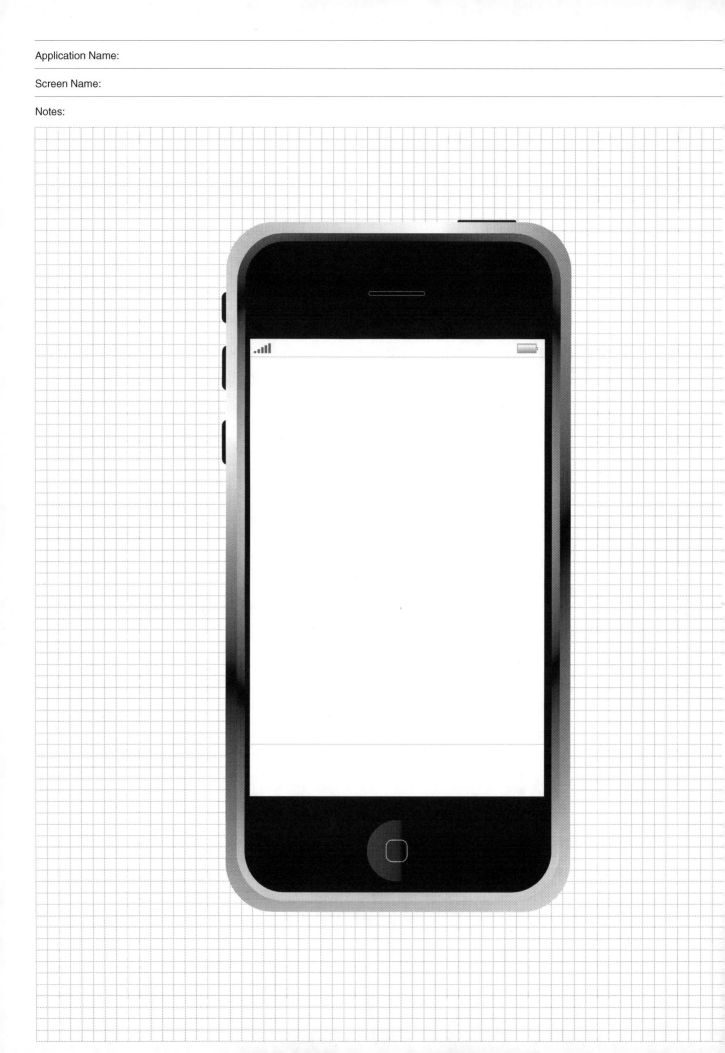

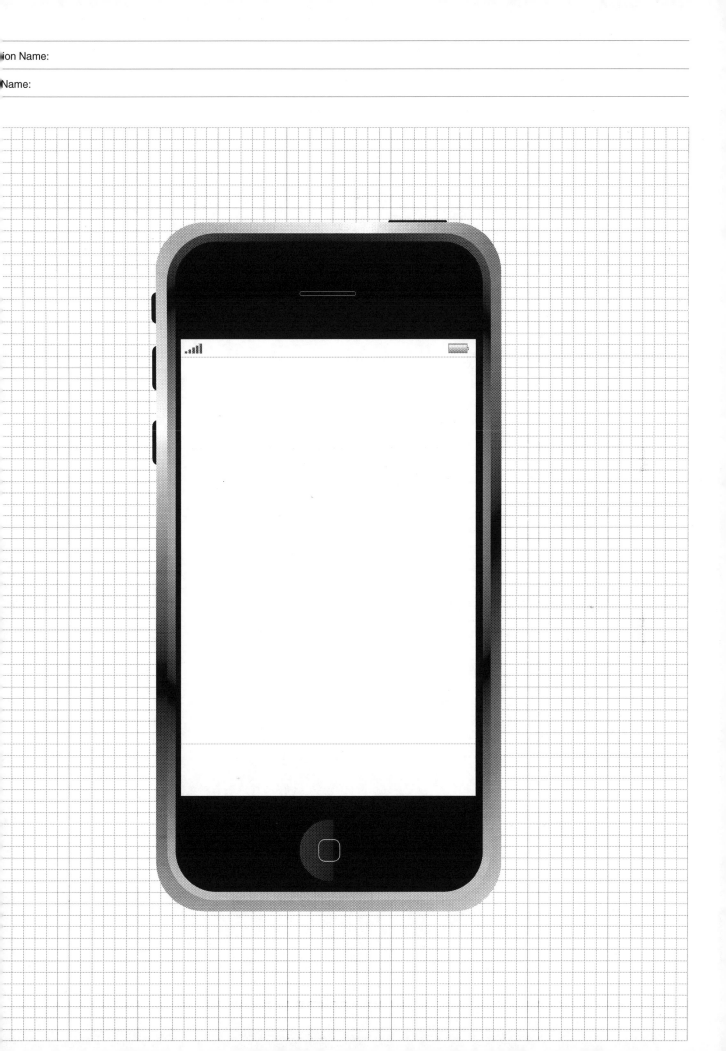

Application Name:

Screen Name:

Notes:

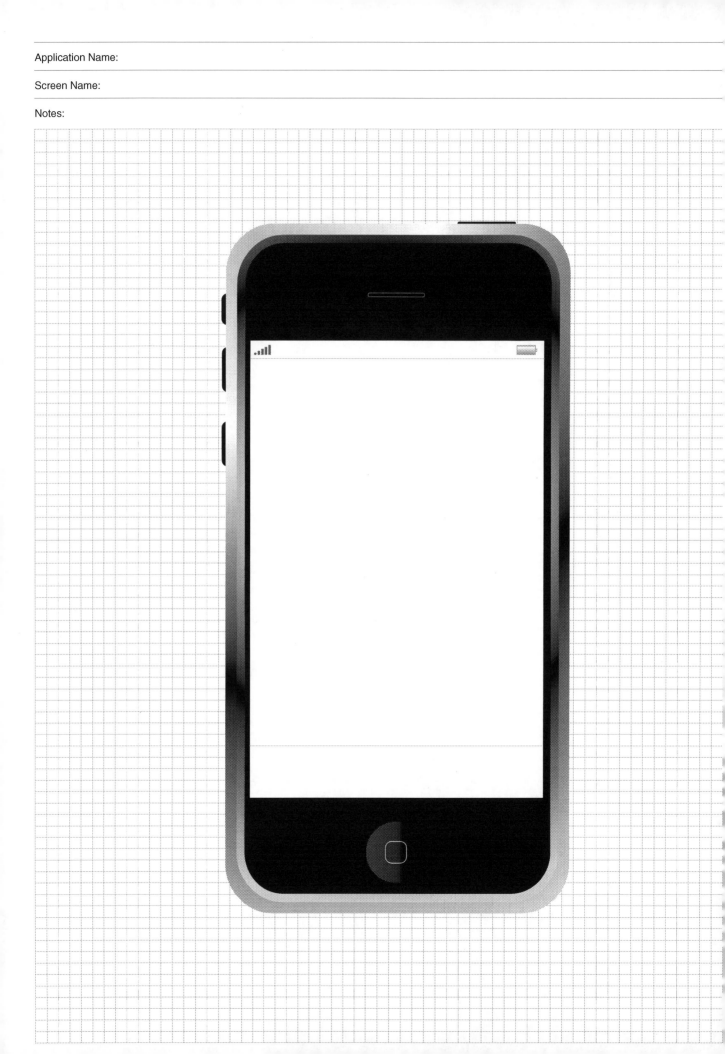

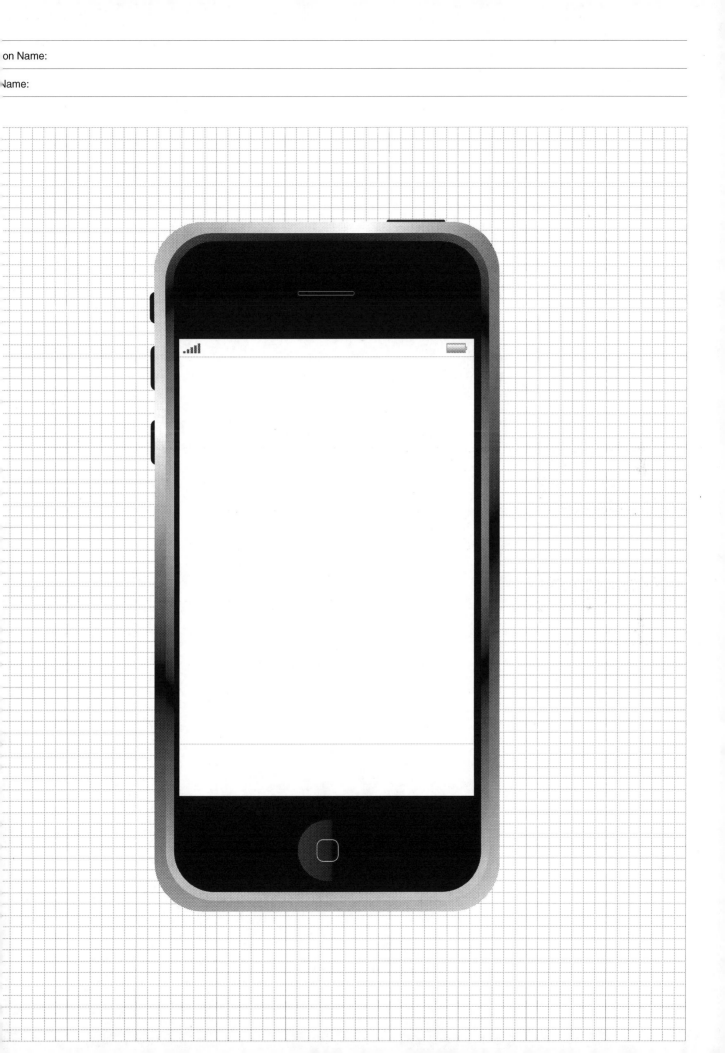

Application Name:

Screen Name:

Notes:

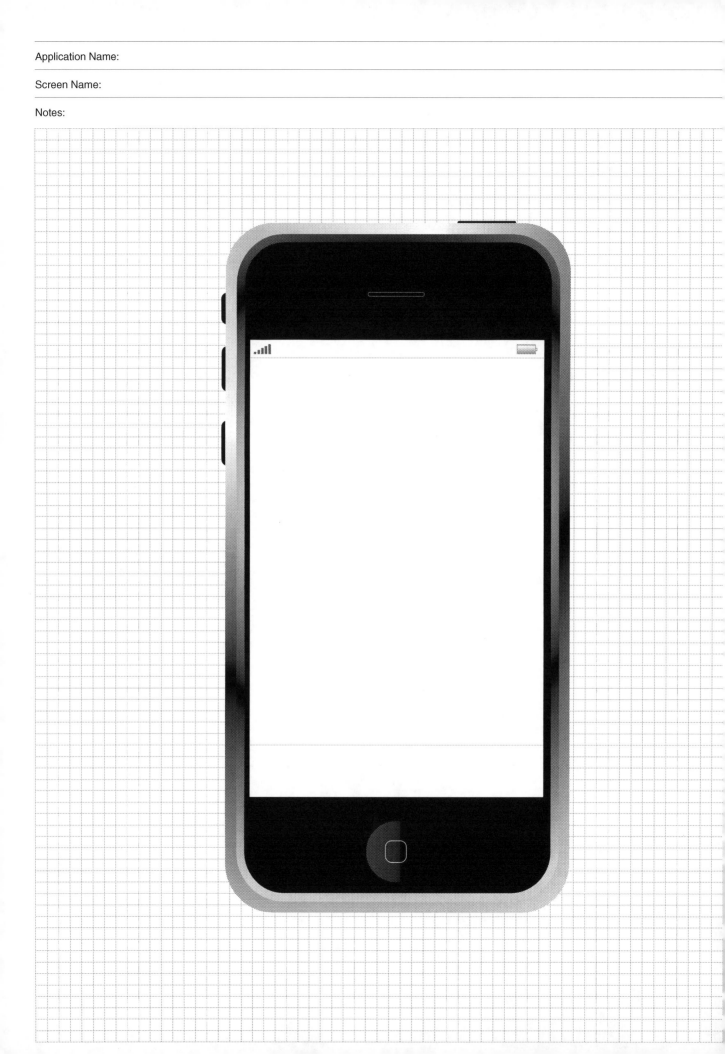

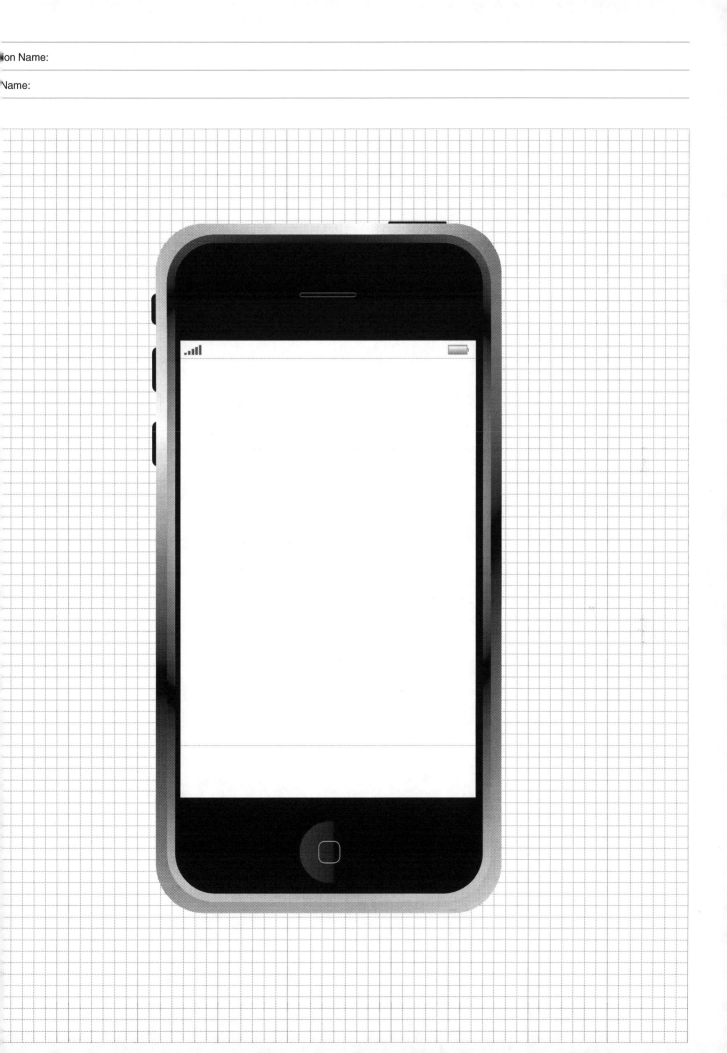

ion Name:

Name:

Application Name:

Screen Name:

Notes:

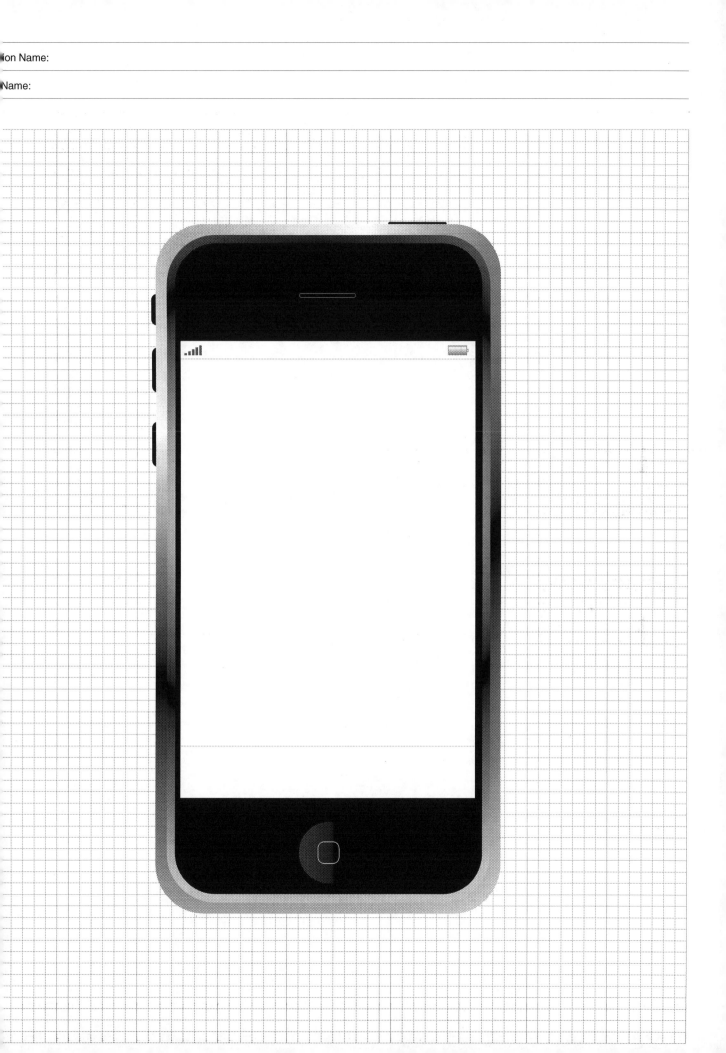

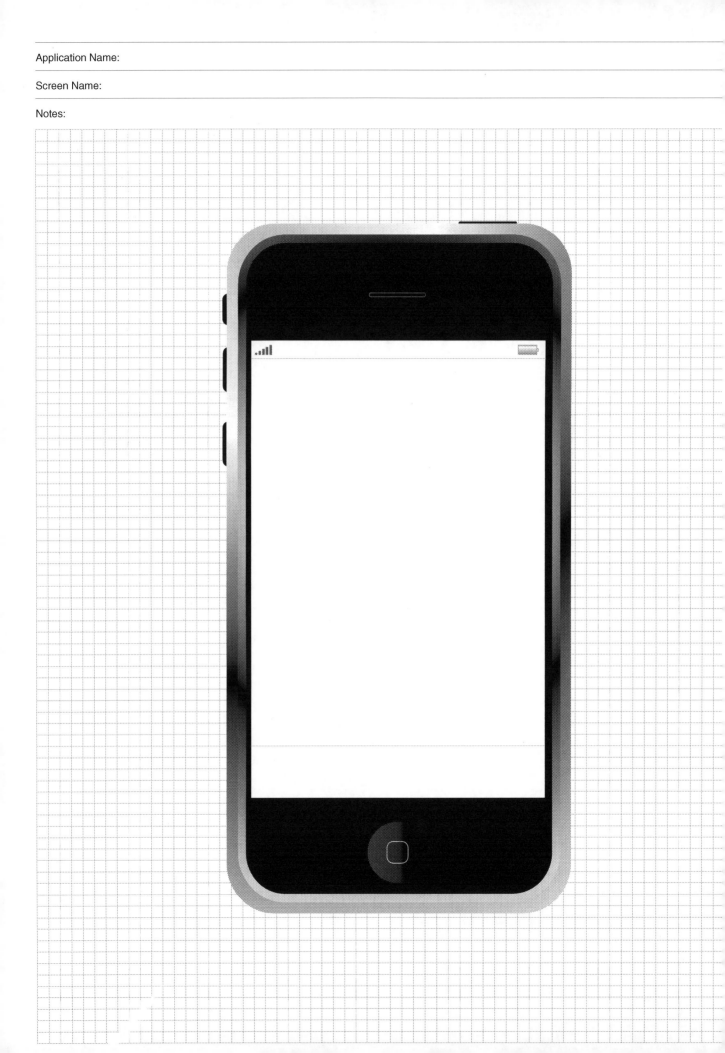

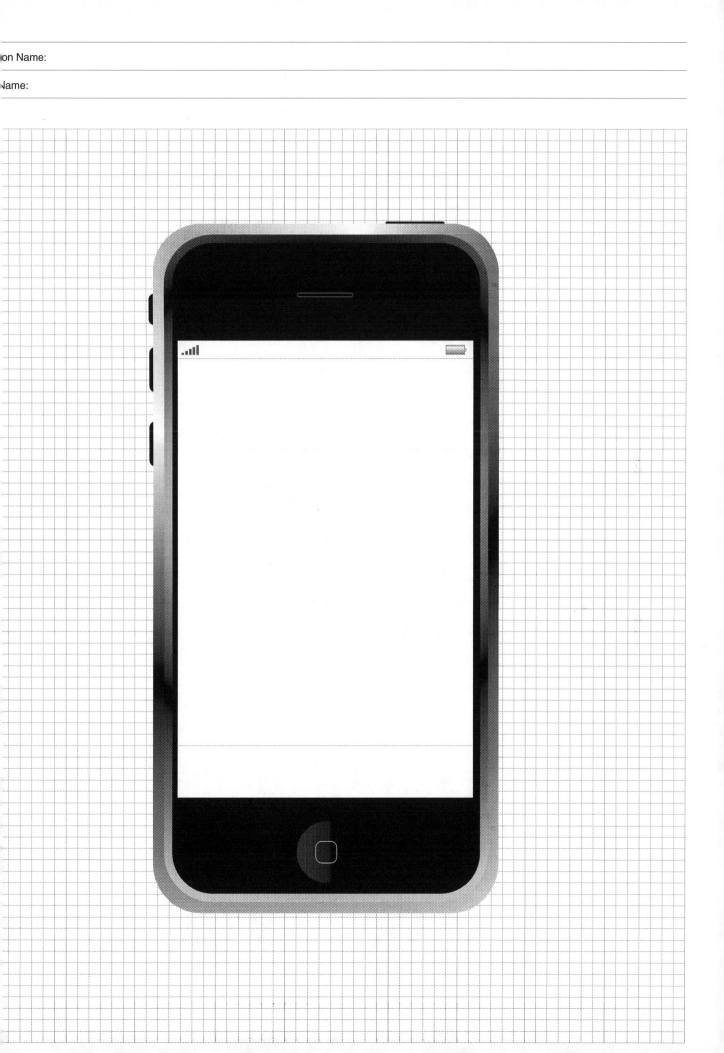

Application Name:

Screen Name:

Notes:

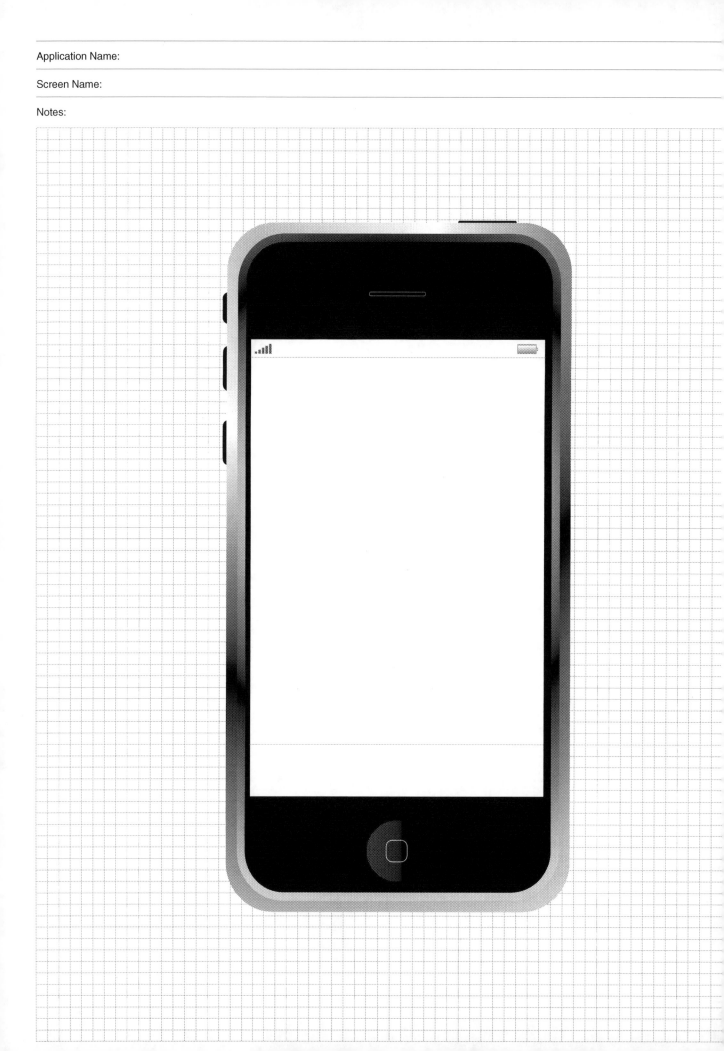

Application Name:

Screen Name:

Notes:

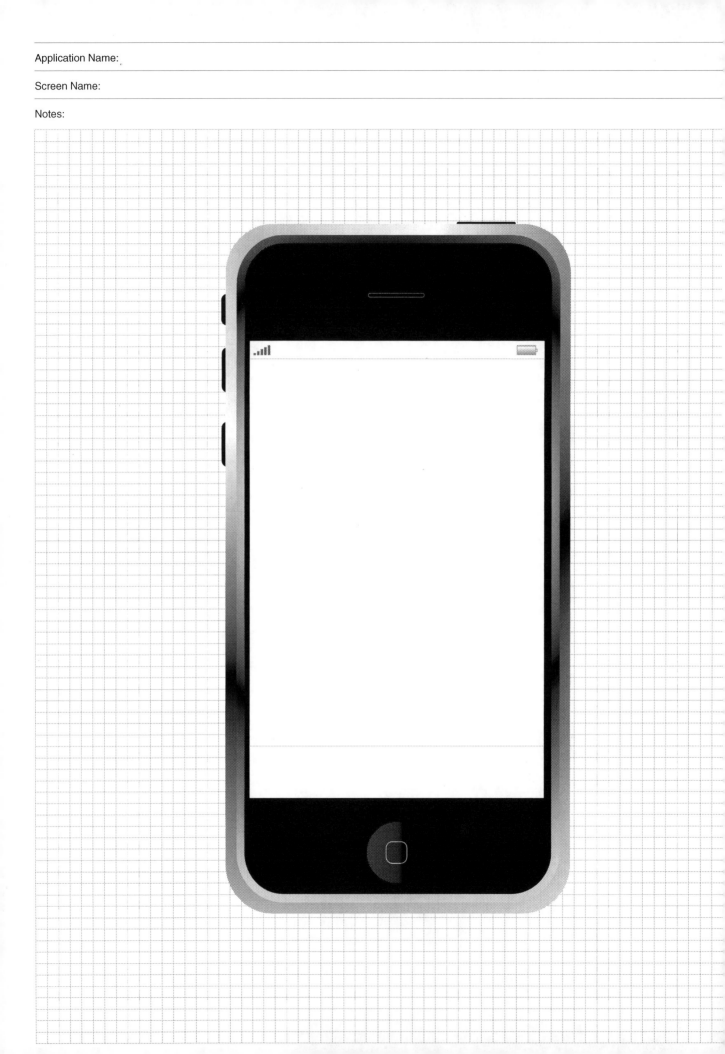

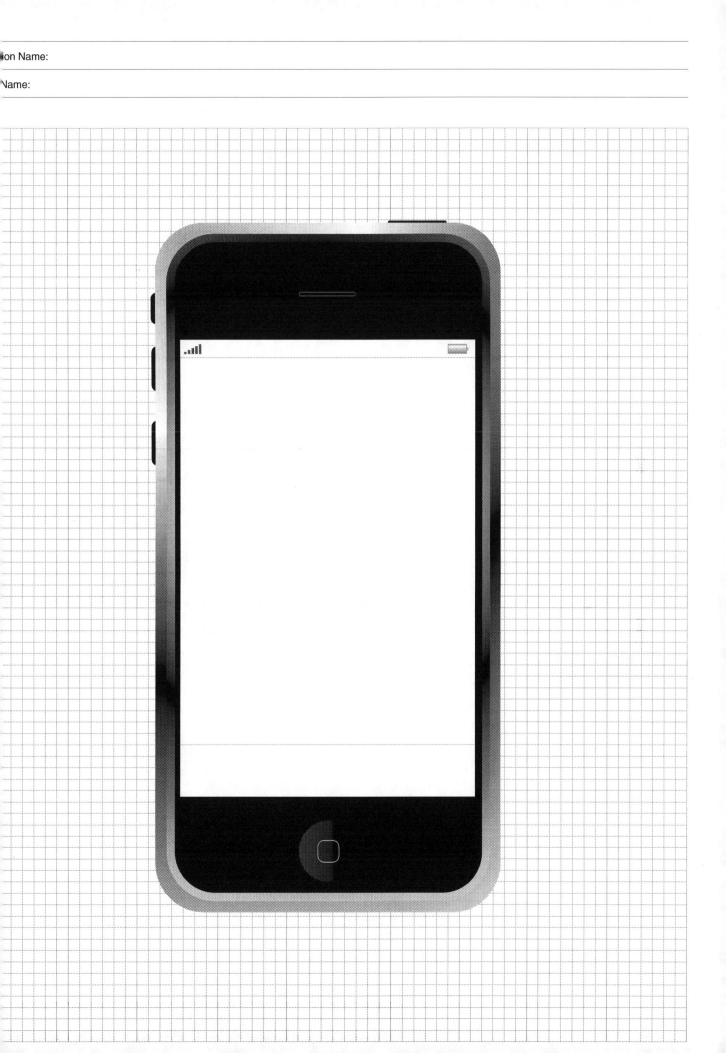

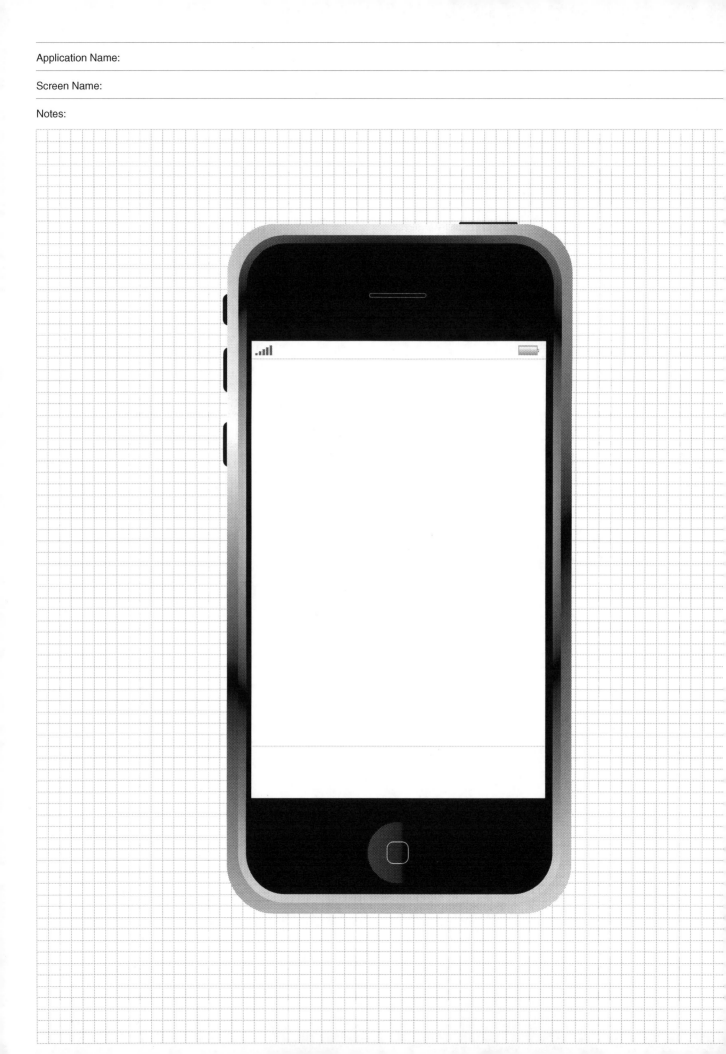

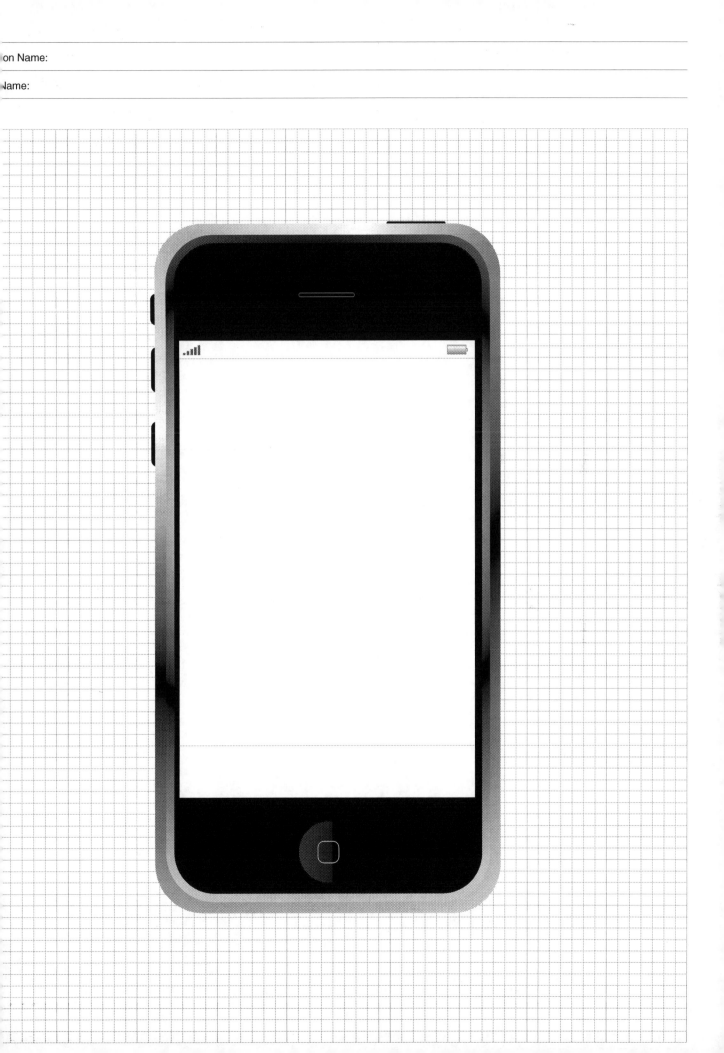

Application Name:

Screen Name:

Notes:

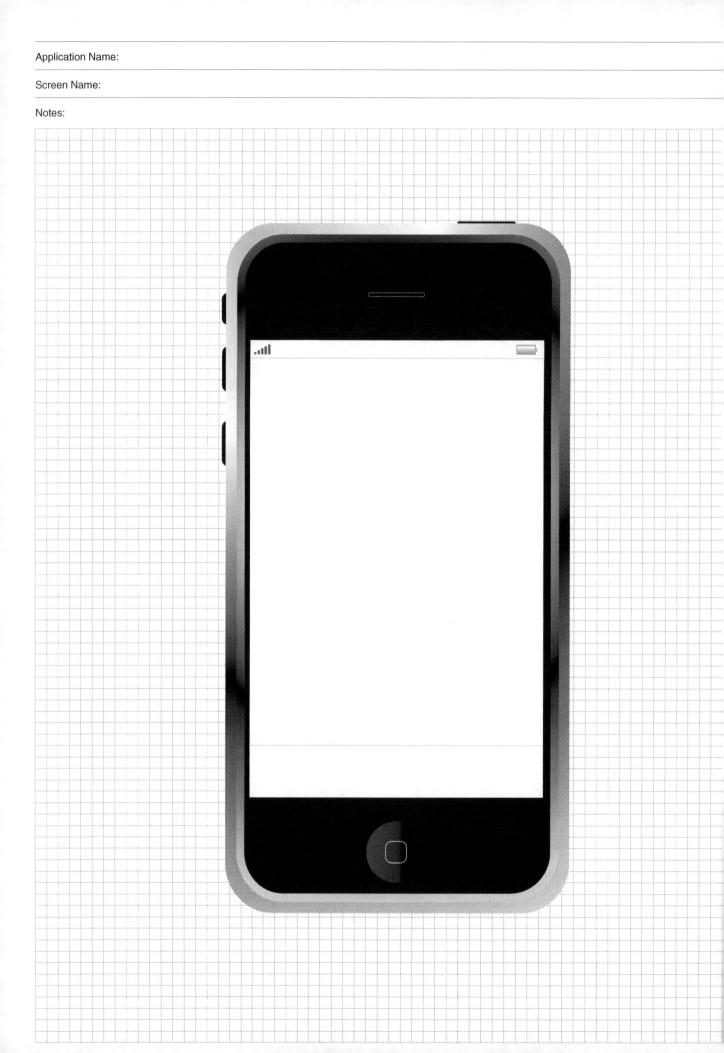

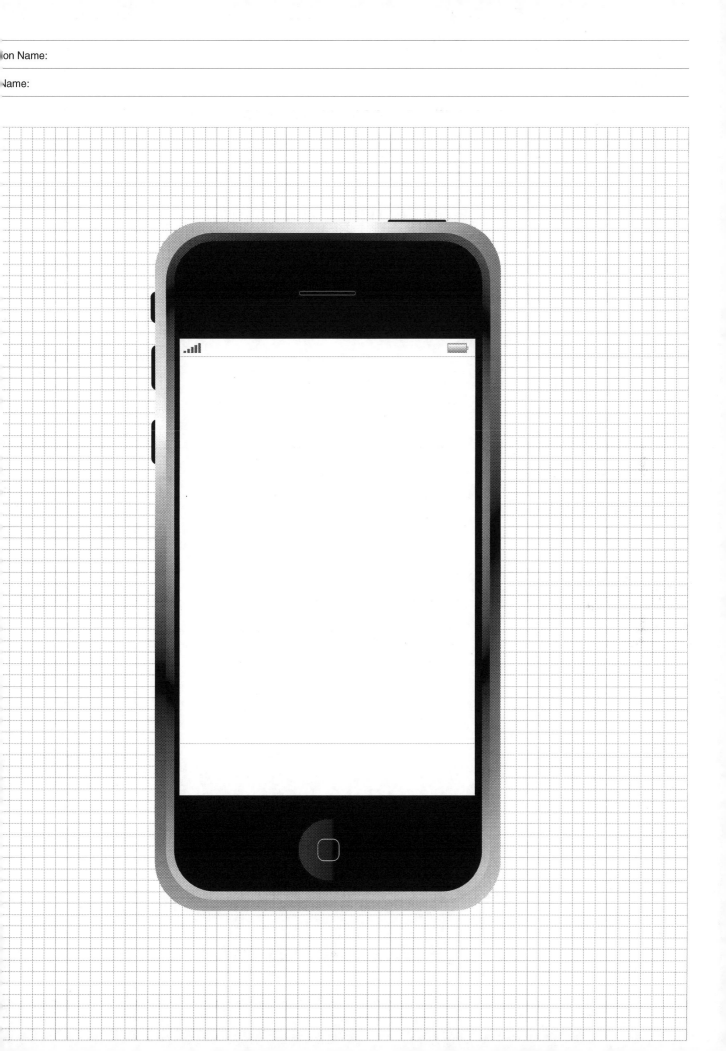

Application Name:

Screen Name:

Notes:

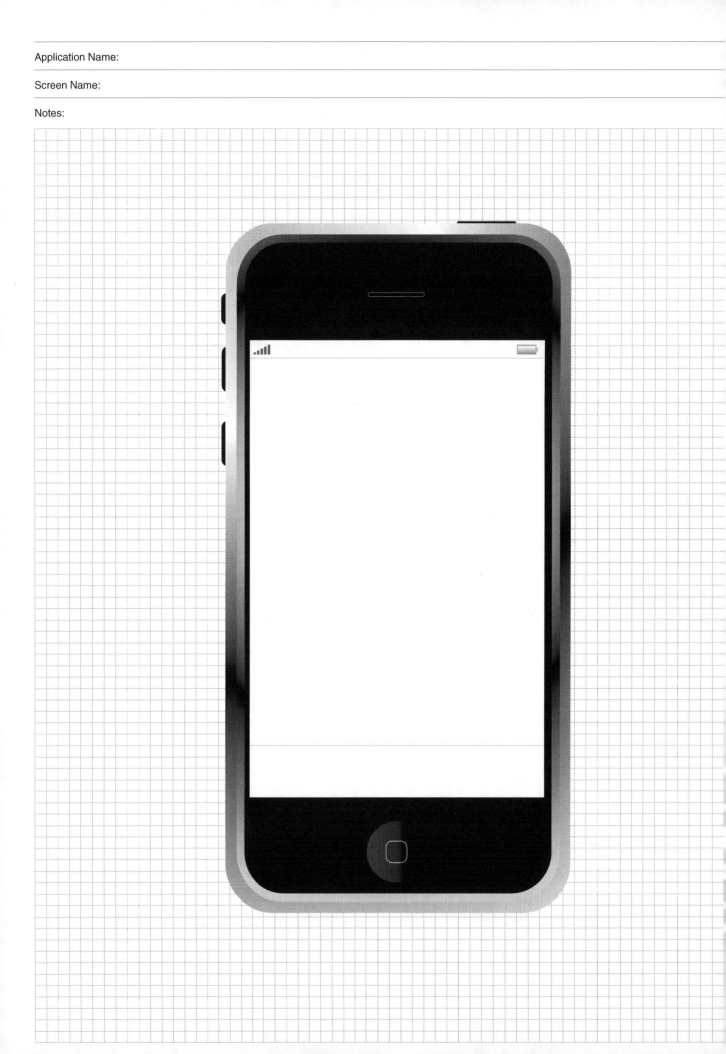

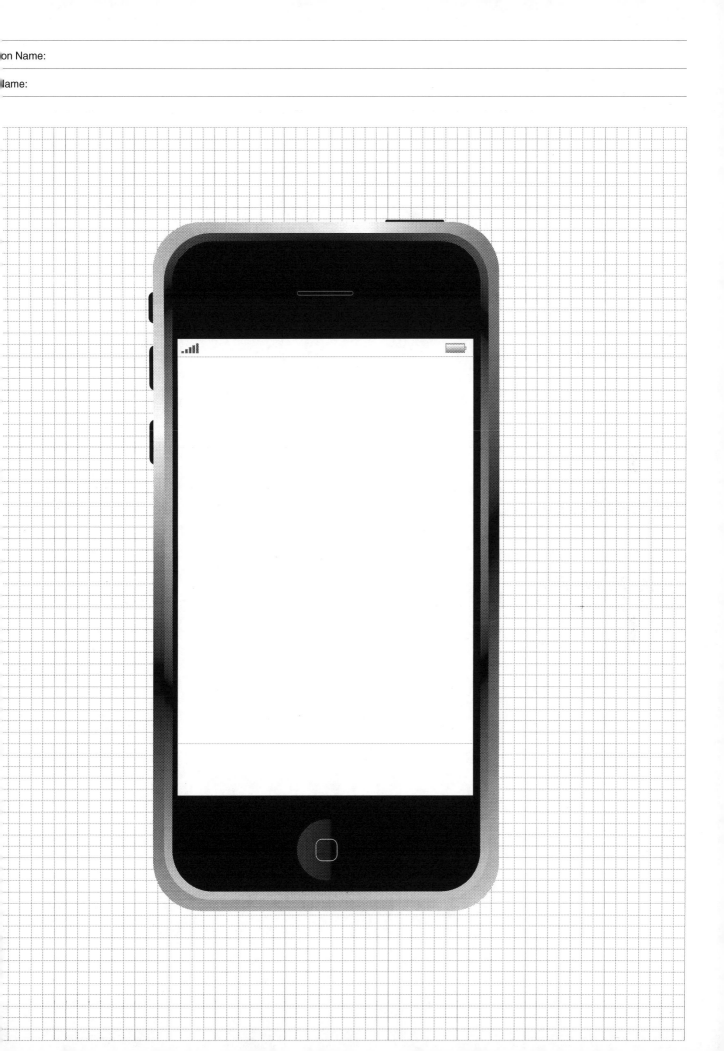

Application Name:

Screen Name:

Notes:

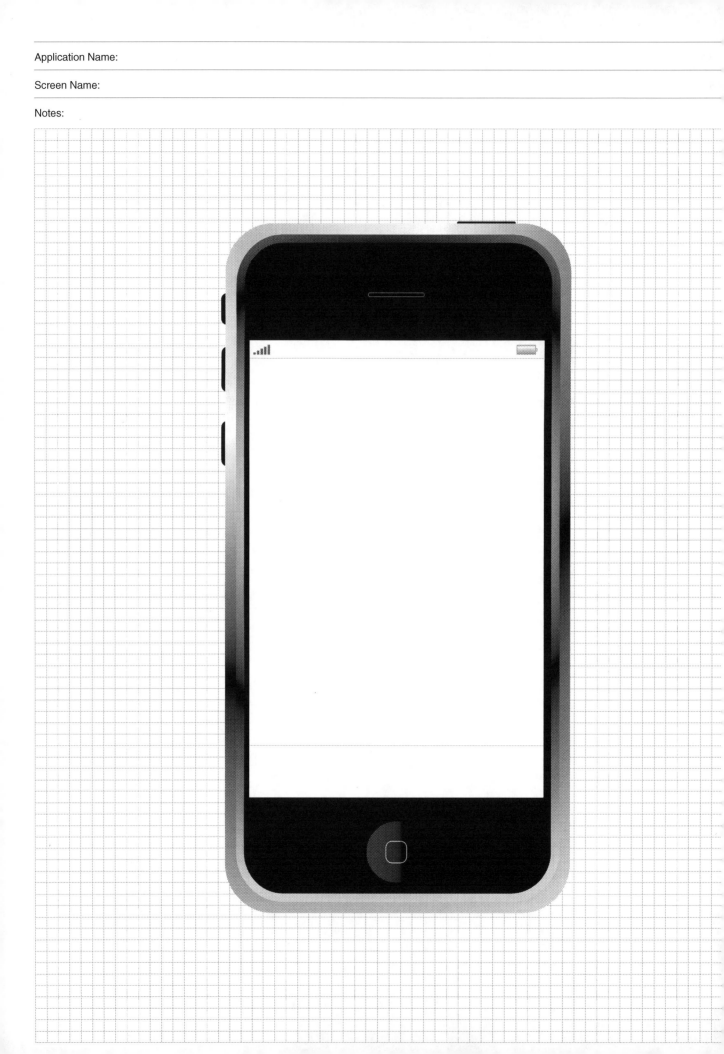

Application Name:

Screen Name:

Notes:

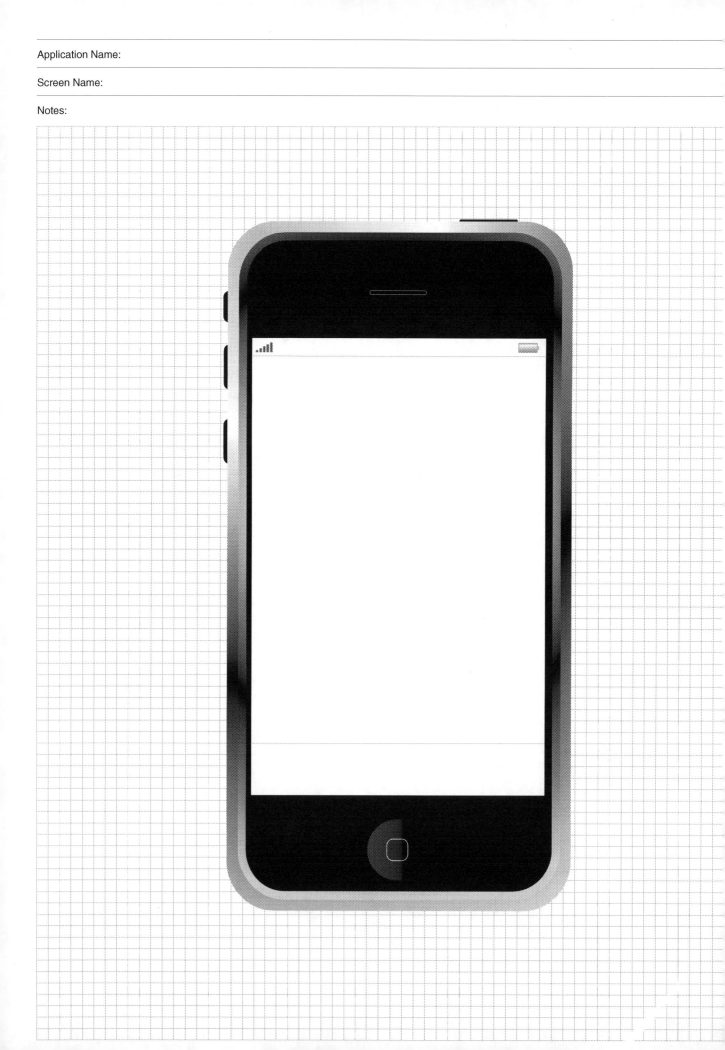

Application Name:

Screen Name:

Notes:

Application Name:

Screen Name:

Notes:

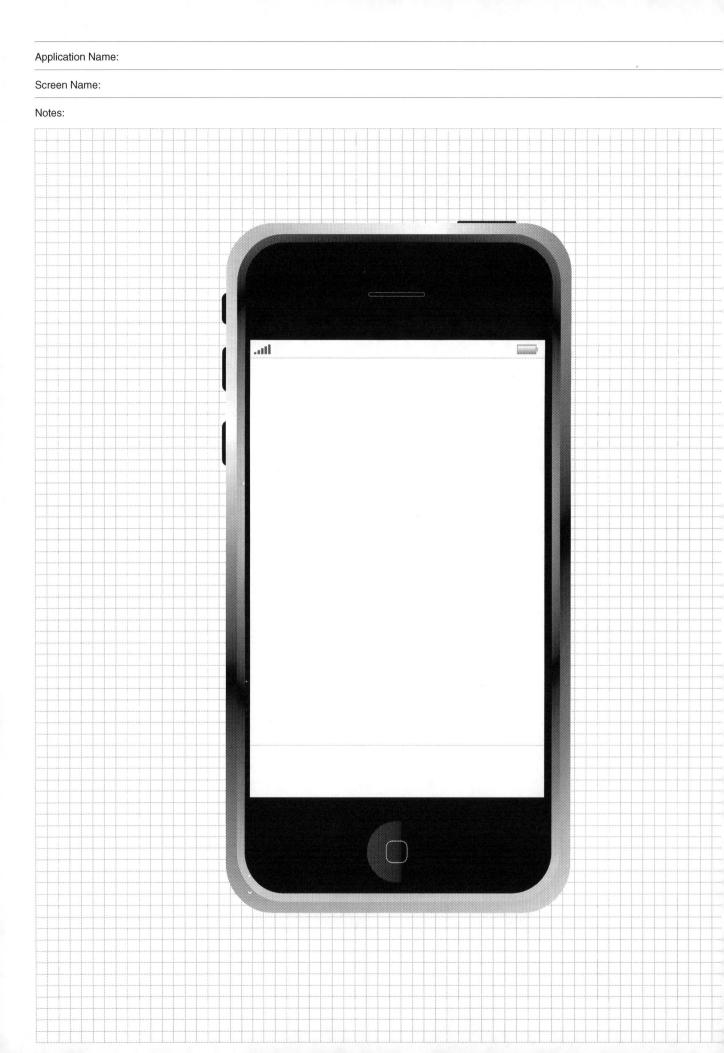

Application Name:

Screen Name:

Notes:

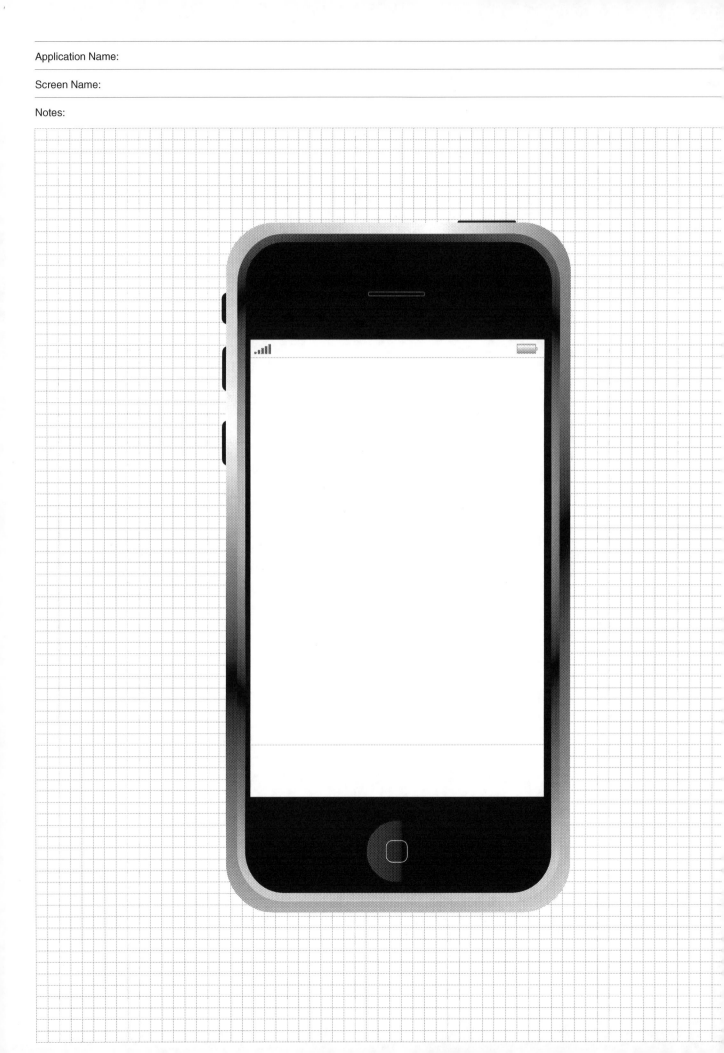

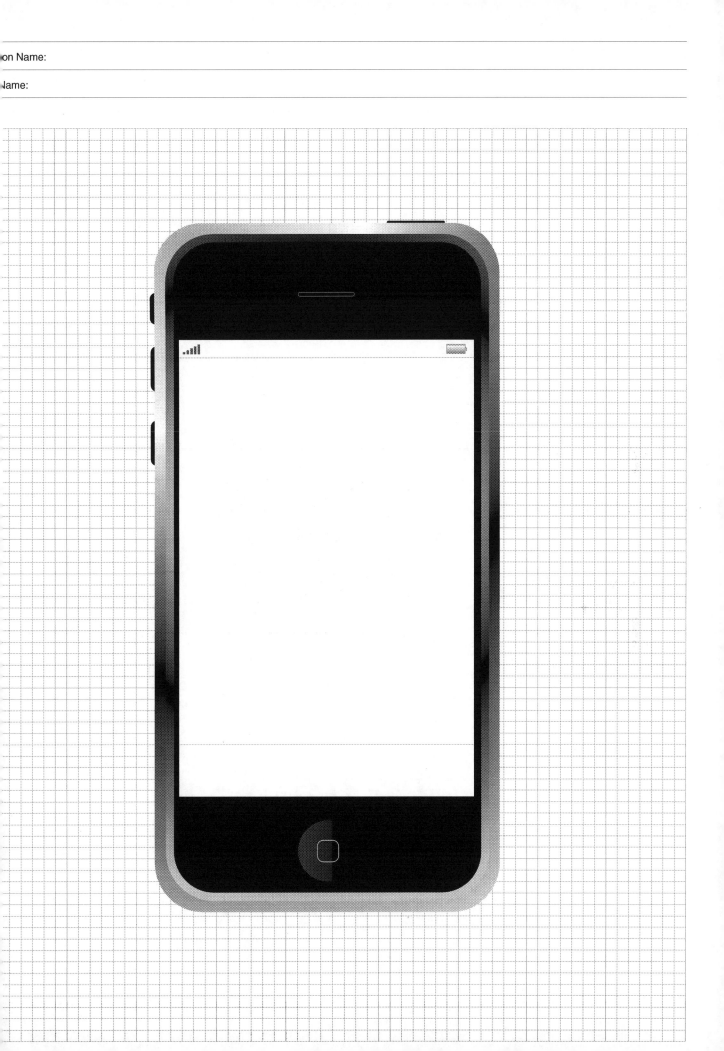

Application Name:

Screen Name:

Notes:

Application Name:

Screen Name:

Notes:

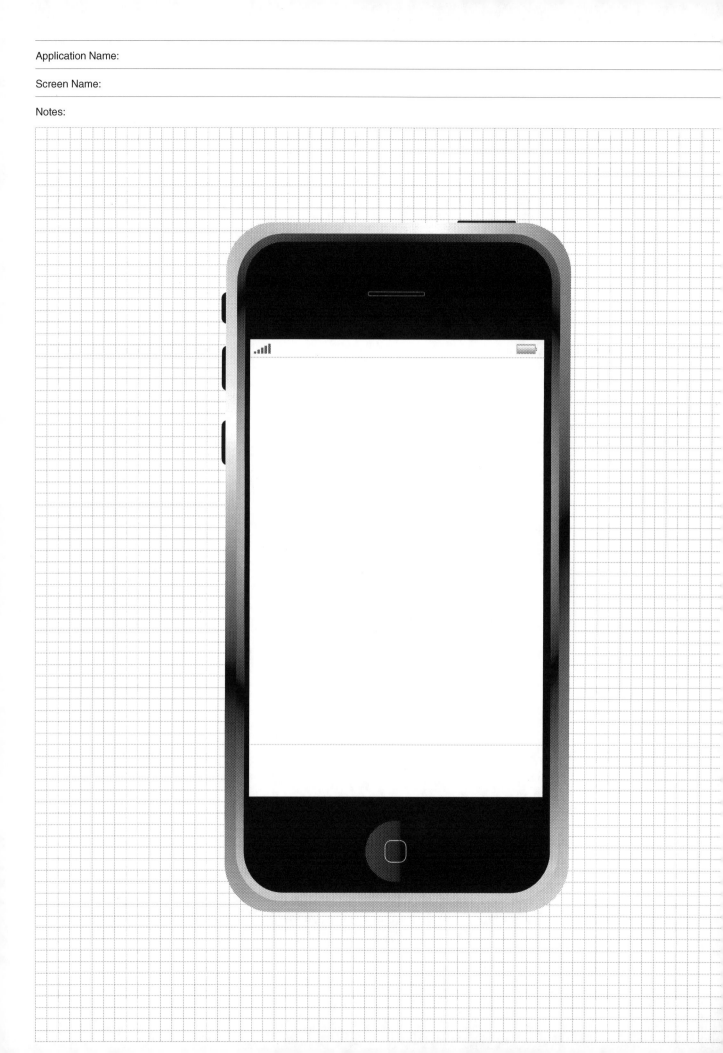

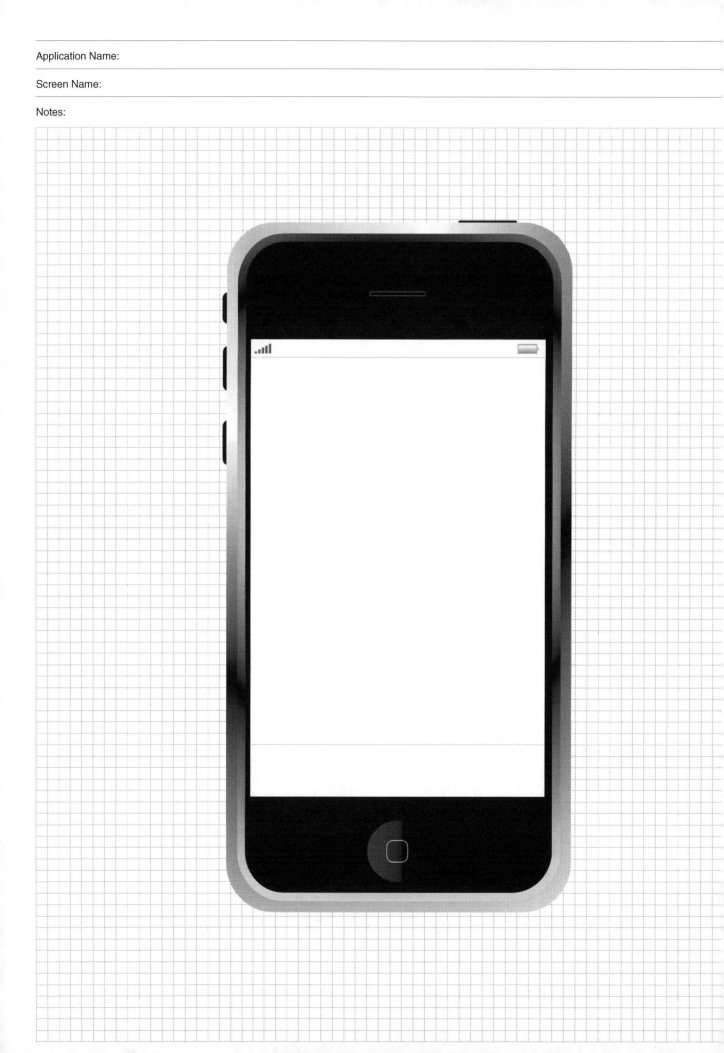

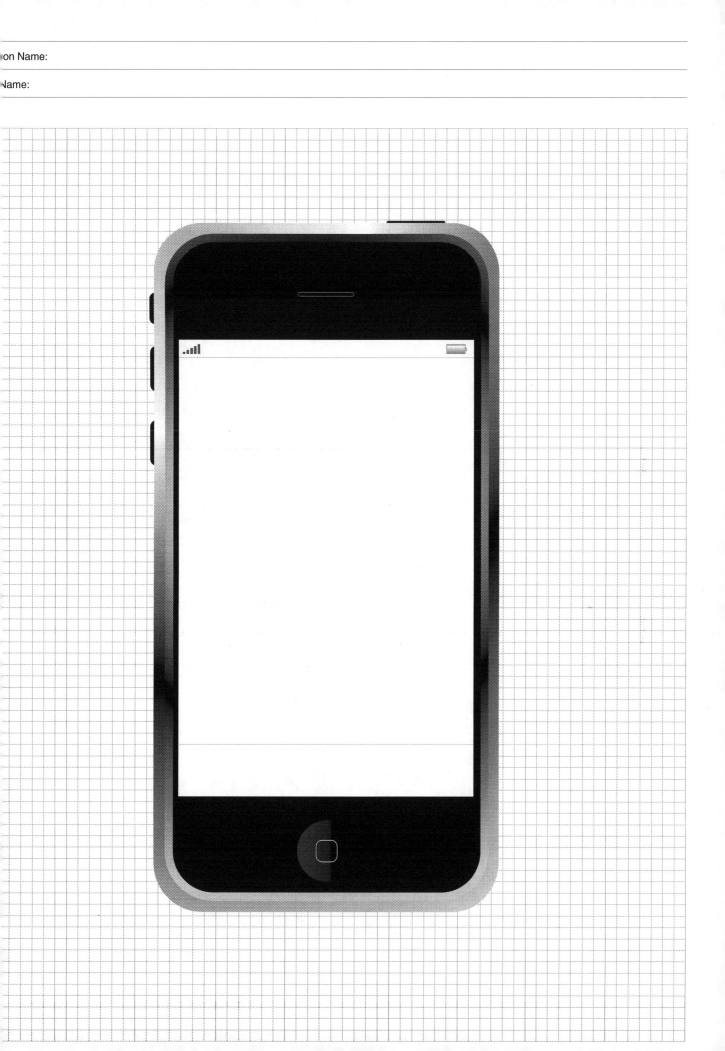

Application Name:

Screen Name:

Notes:

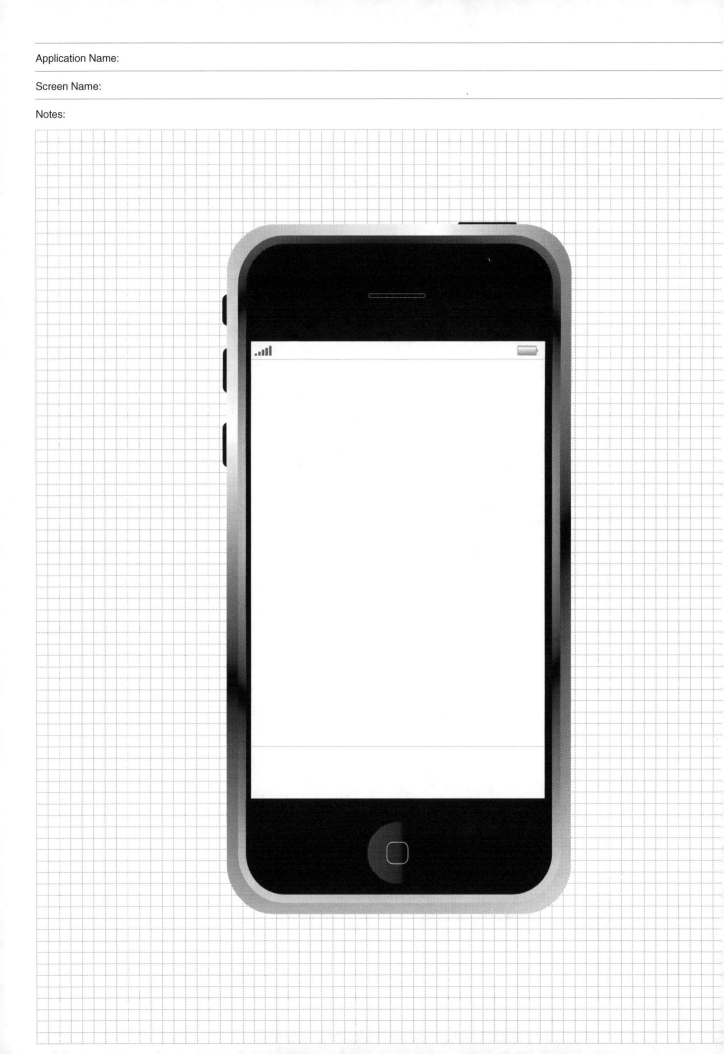

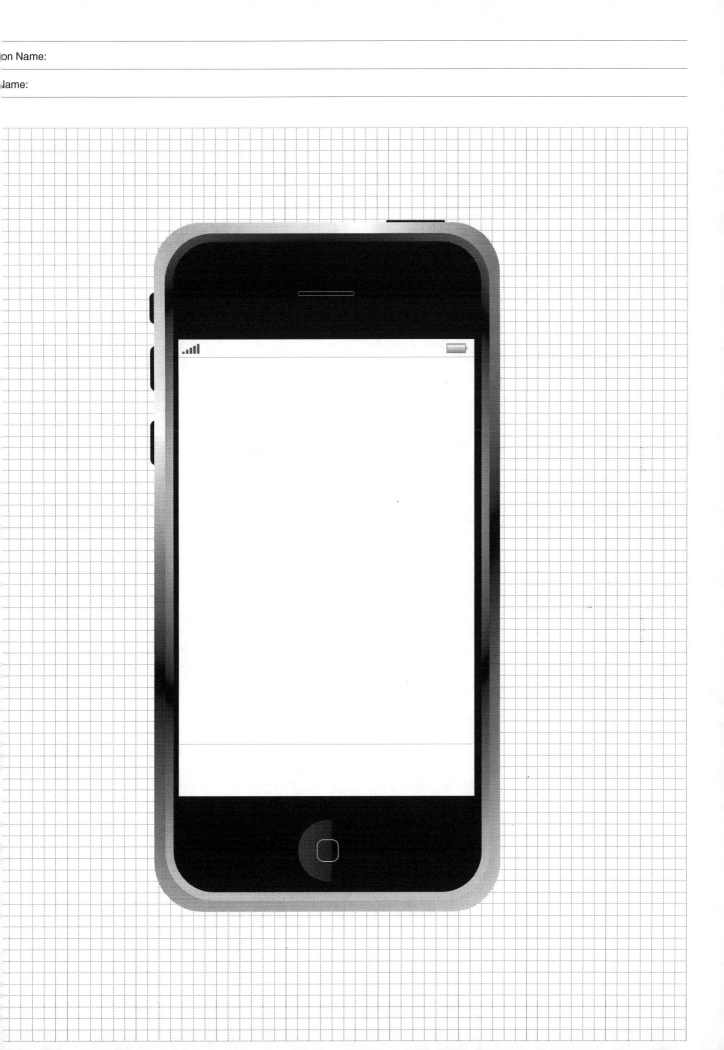

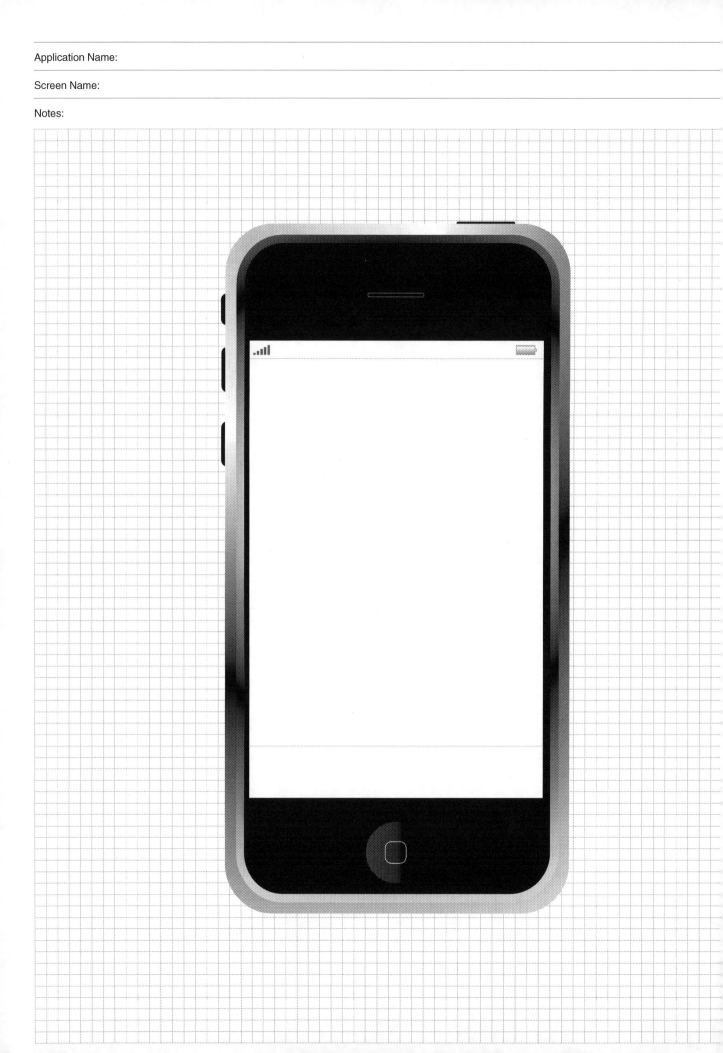

Application Name:

Screen Name:

Notes:

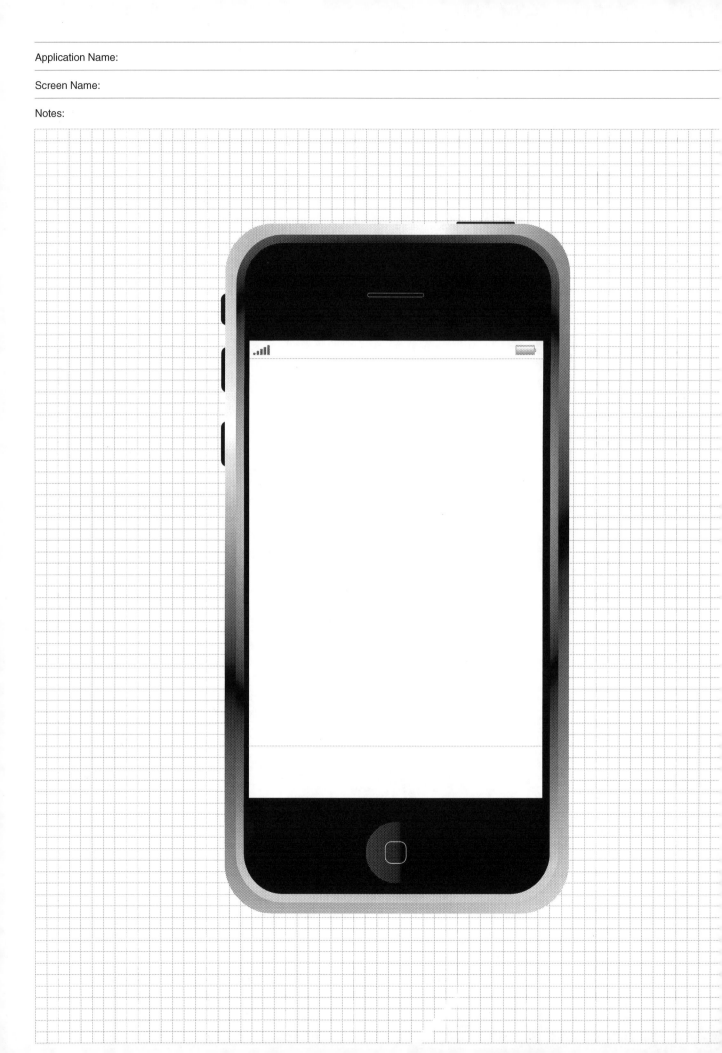

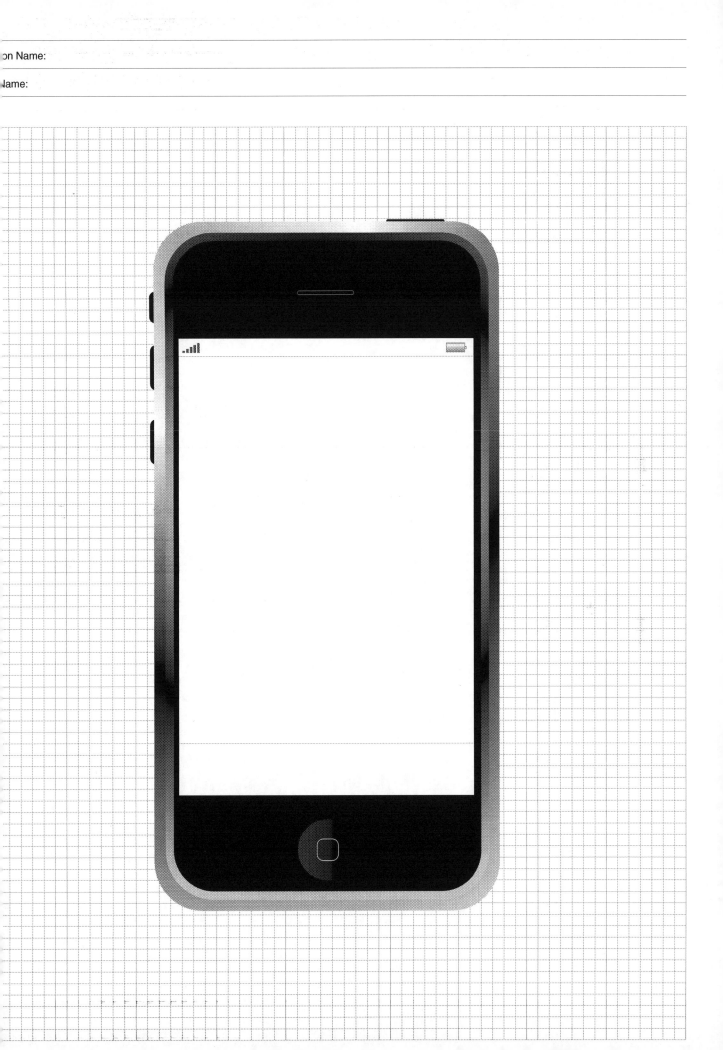

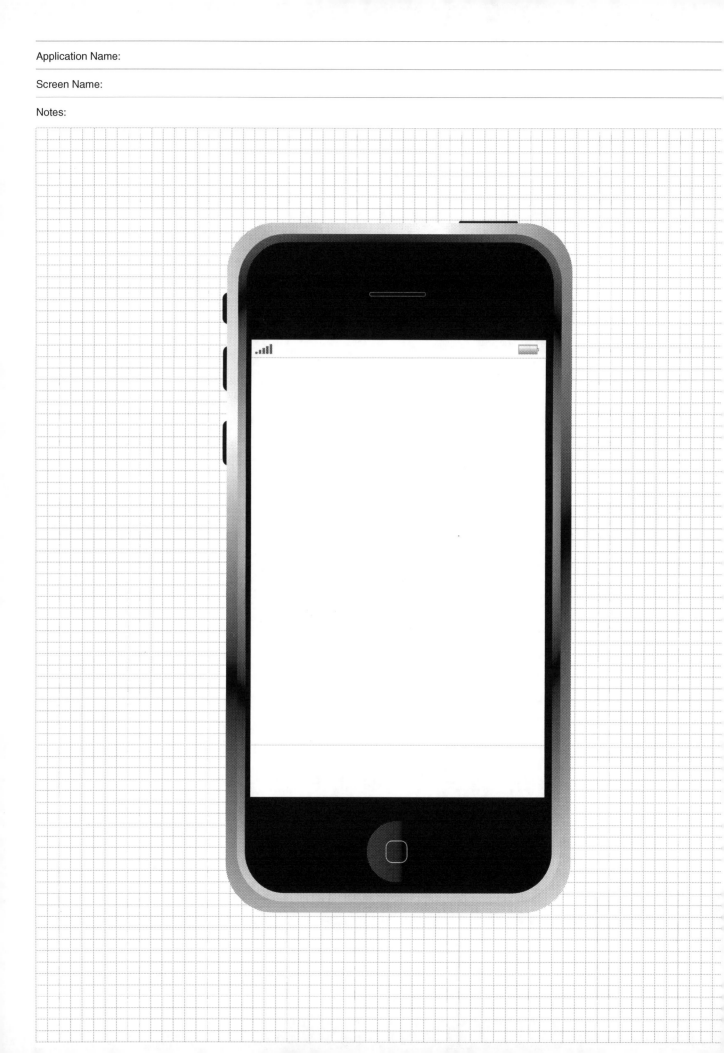

Application Name:

Screen Name:

Notes:

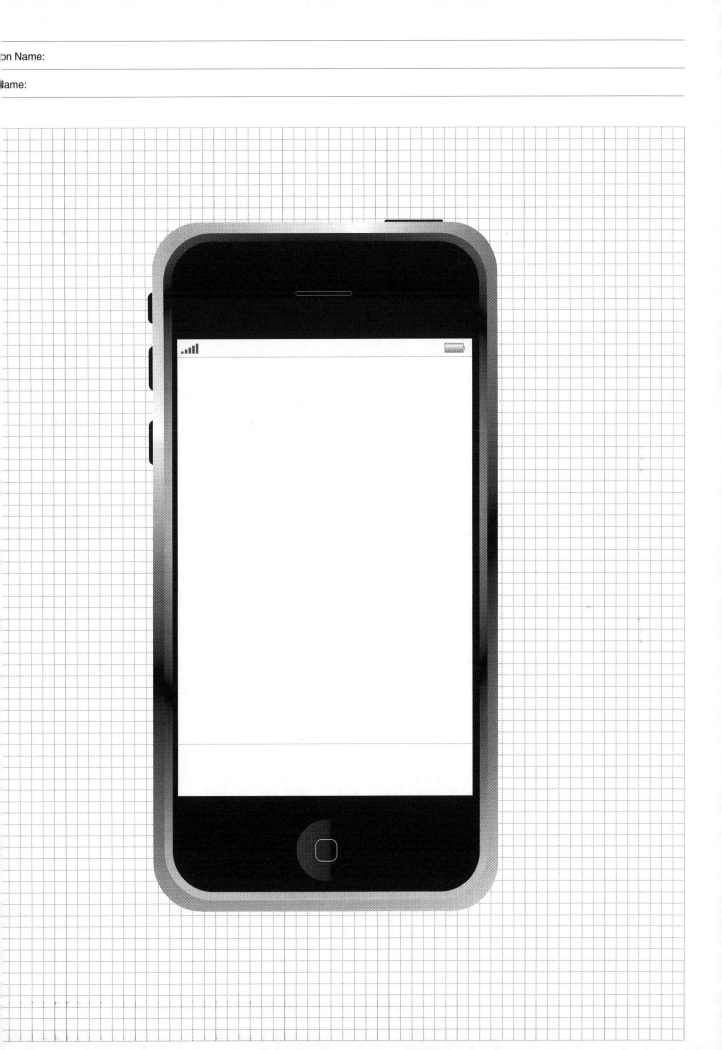

Application Name:

Screen Name:

Notes:

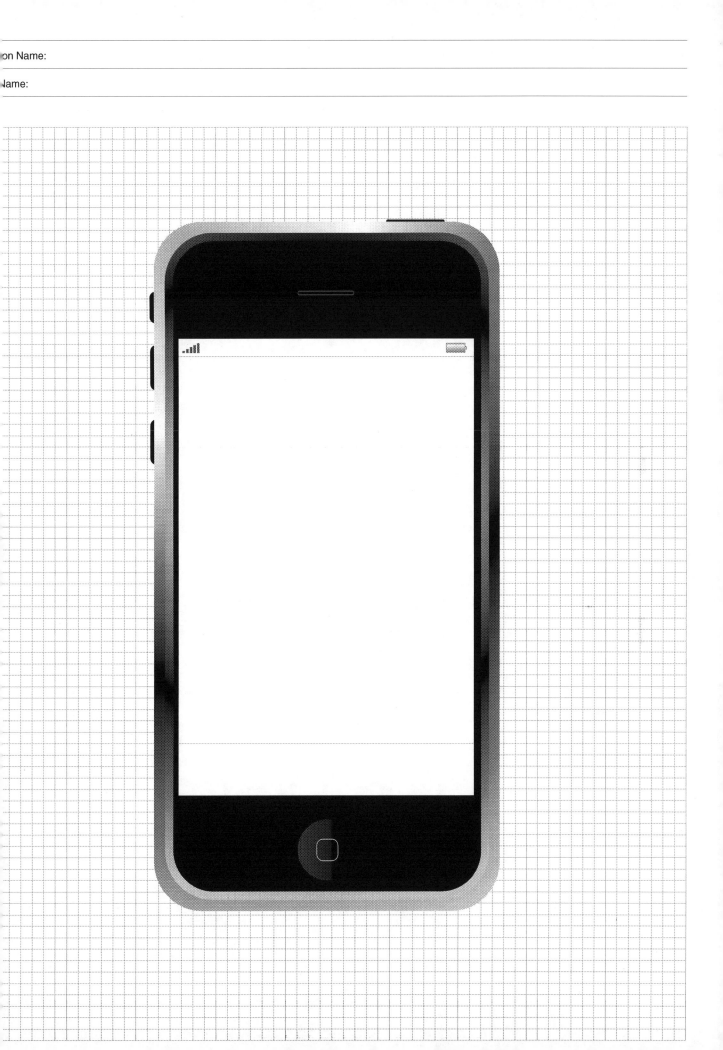

Application Name:

Screen Name:

Notes:

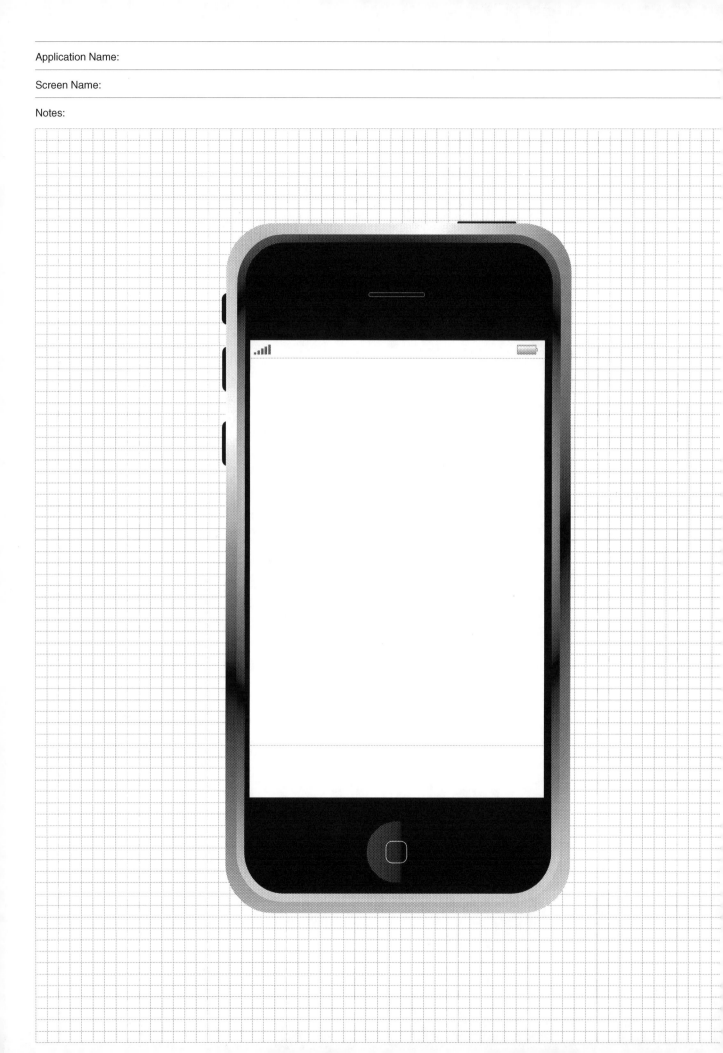

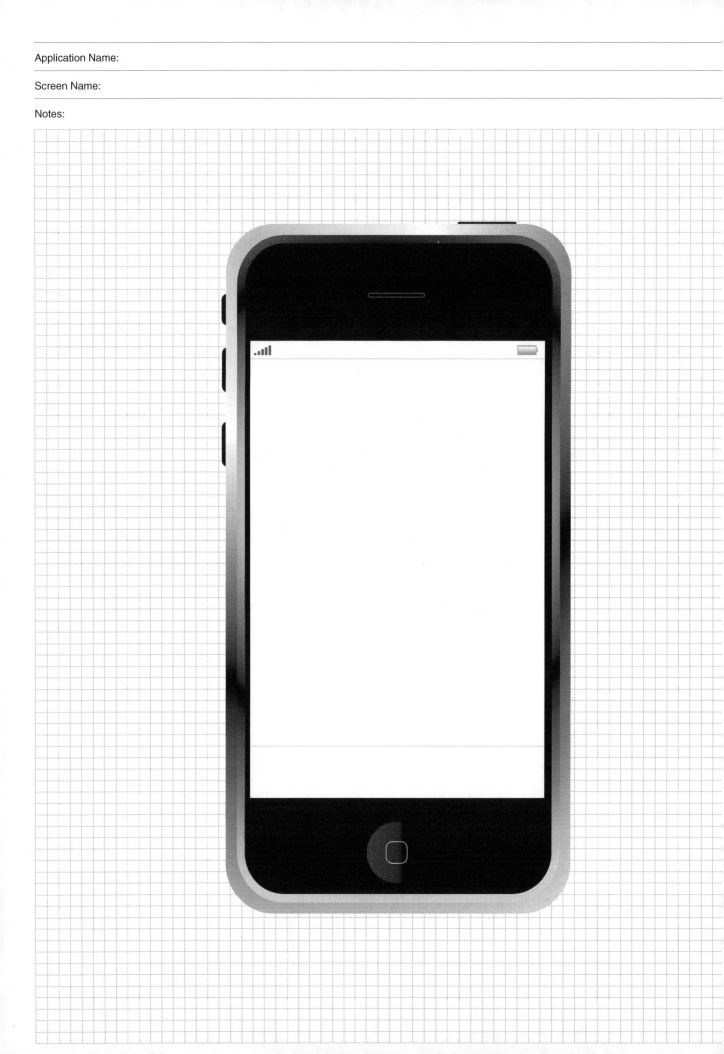

Application Name:

Screen Name:

Notes:

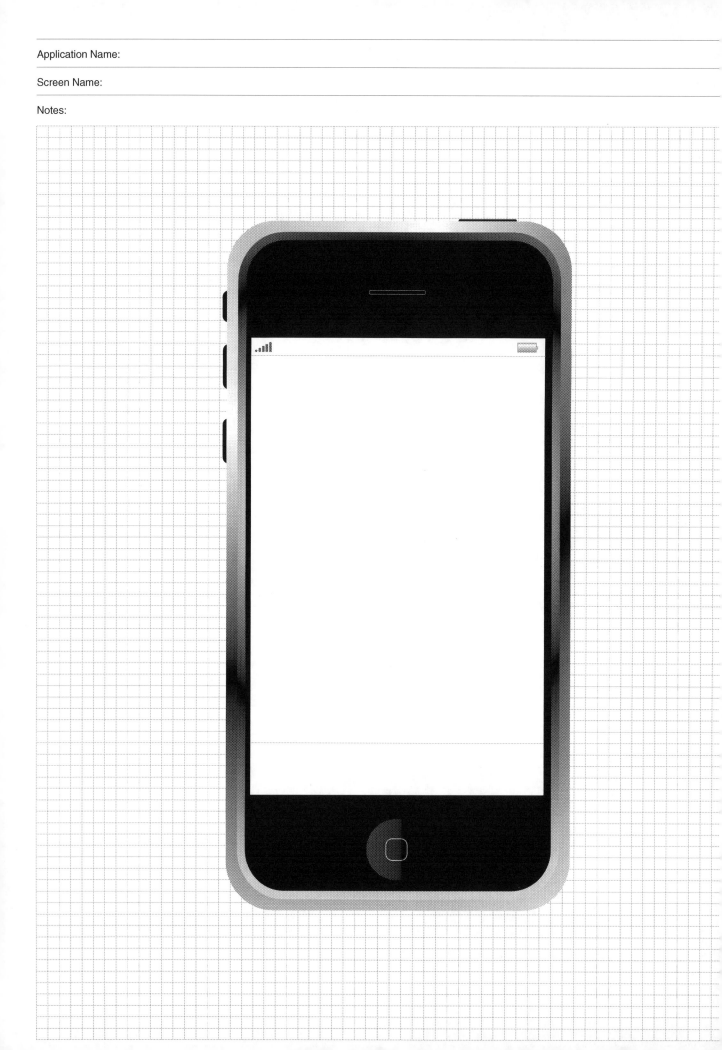

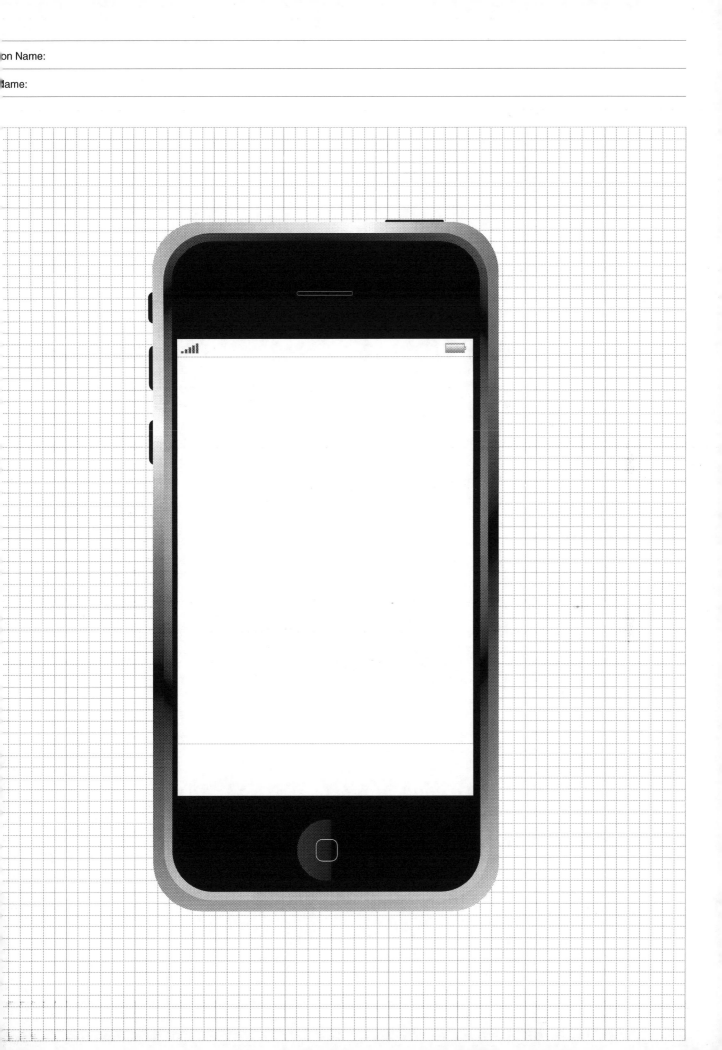

Application Name:

Screen Name:

Notes:

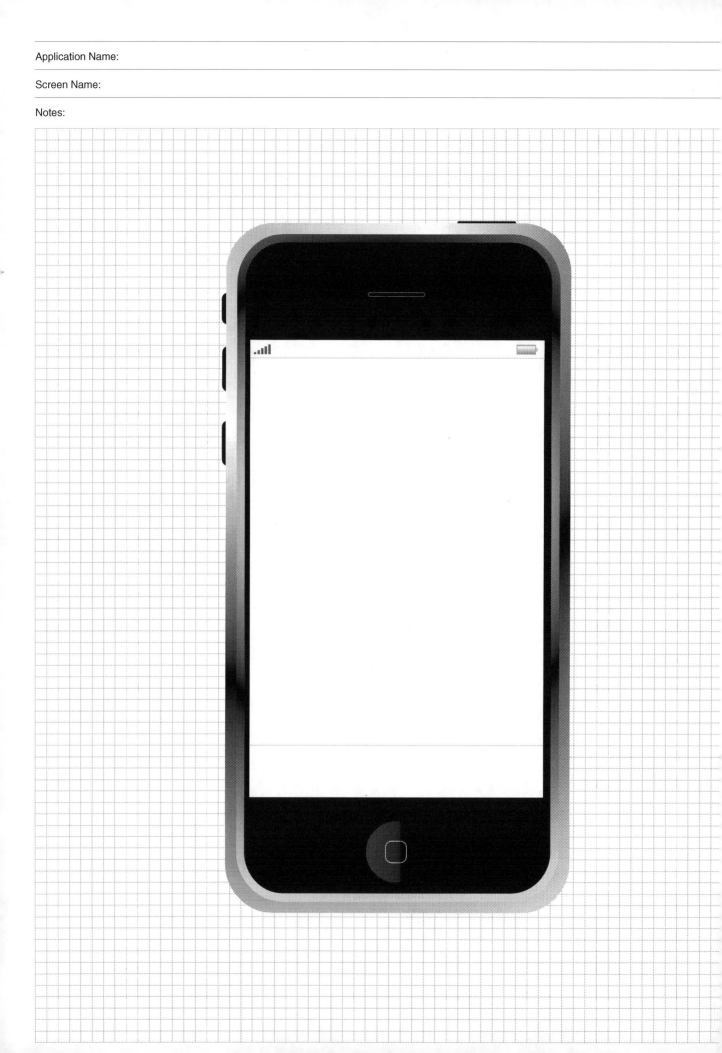

Application Name:

Screen Name:

Notes:

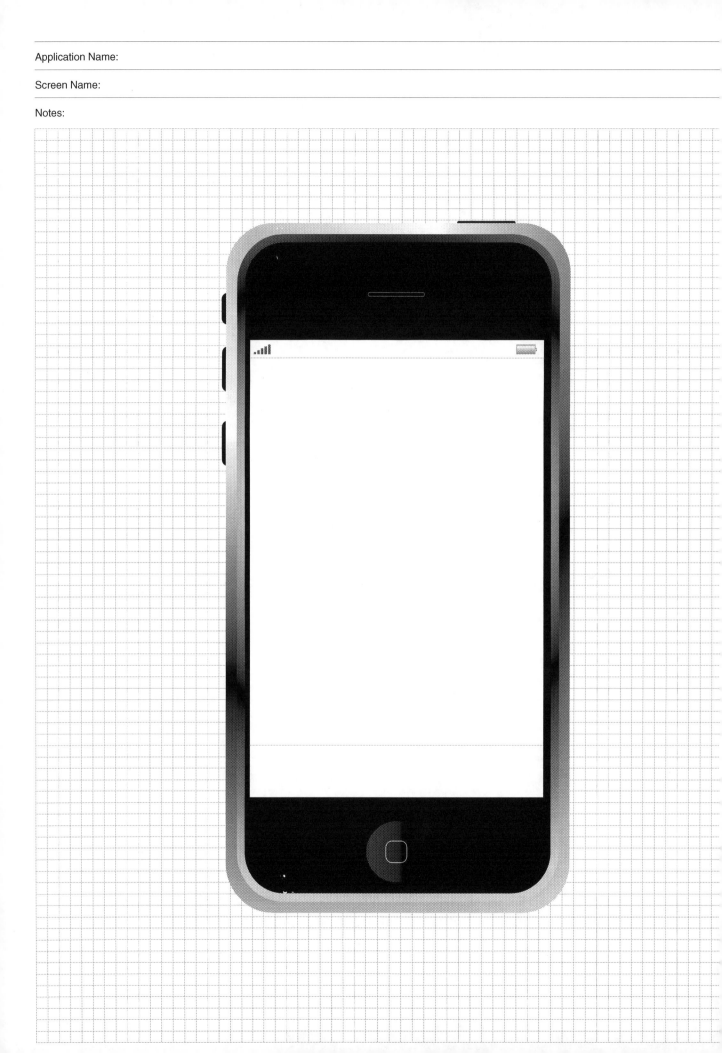

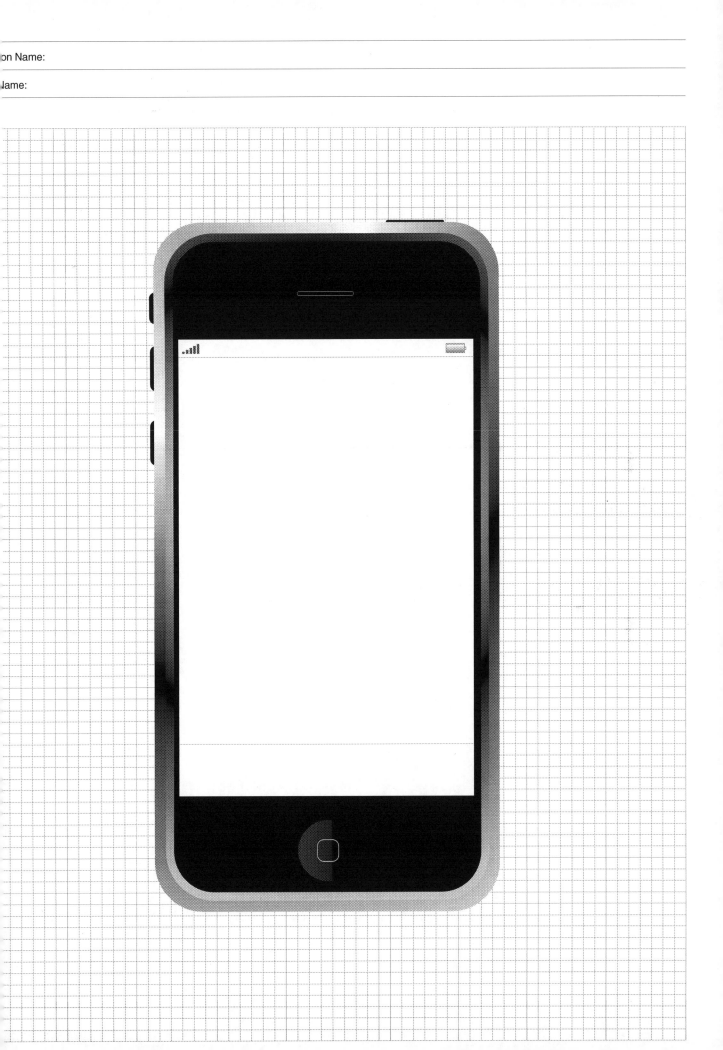

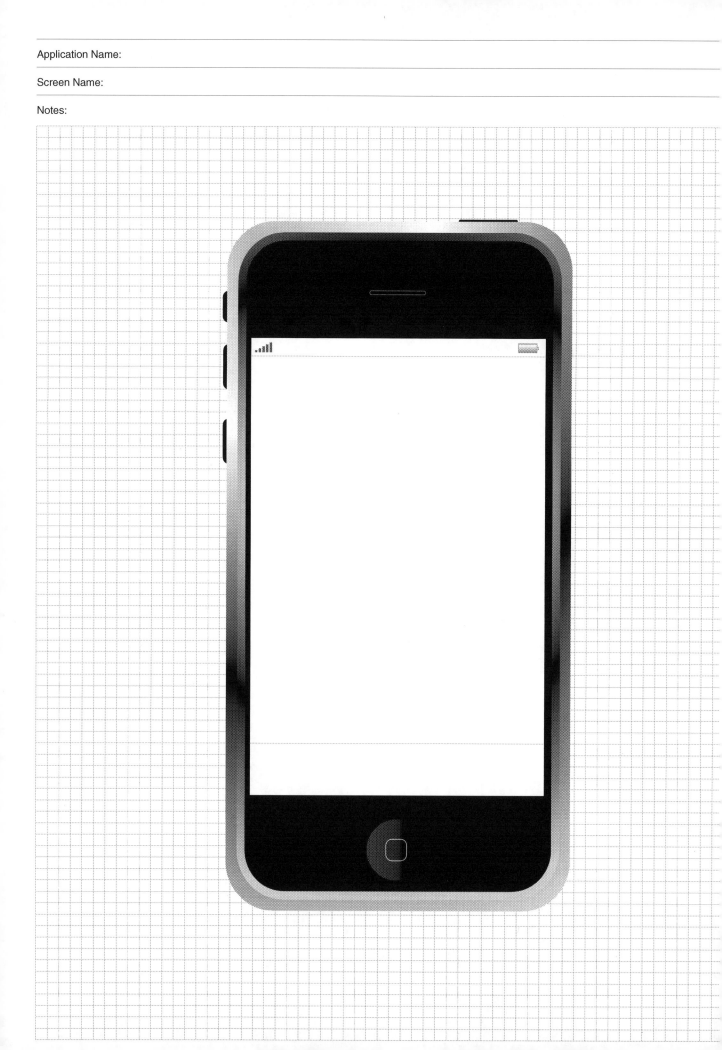

Application Name:

Screen Name:

Notes:

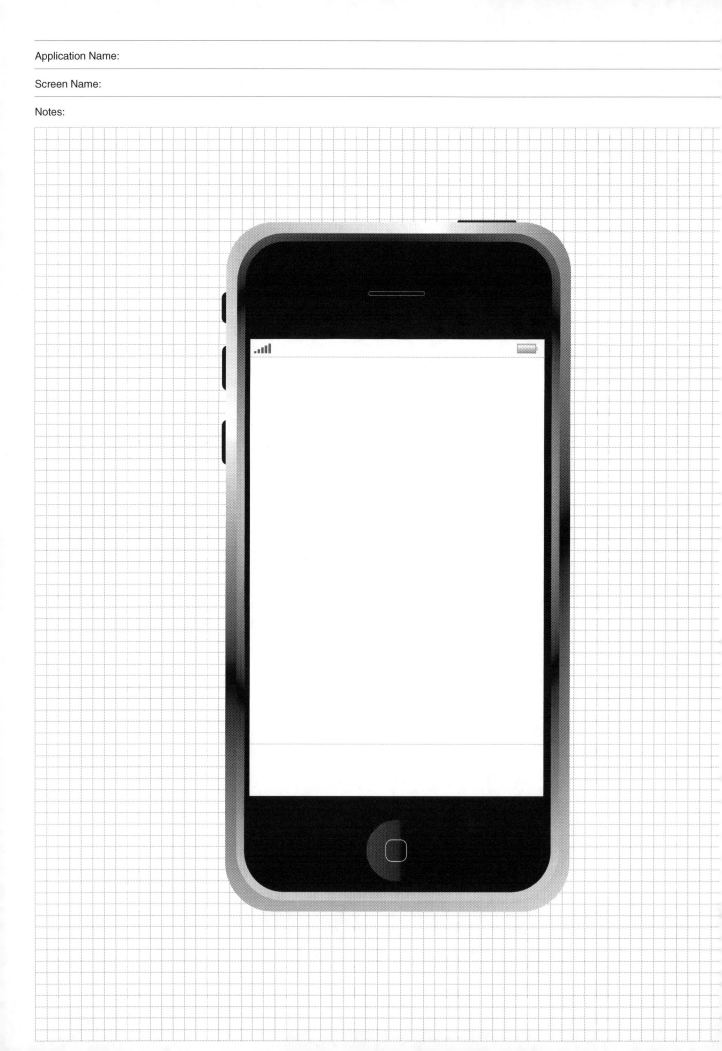

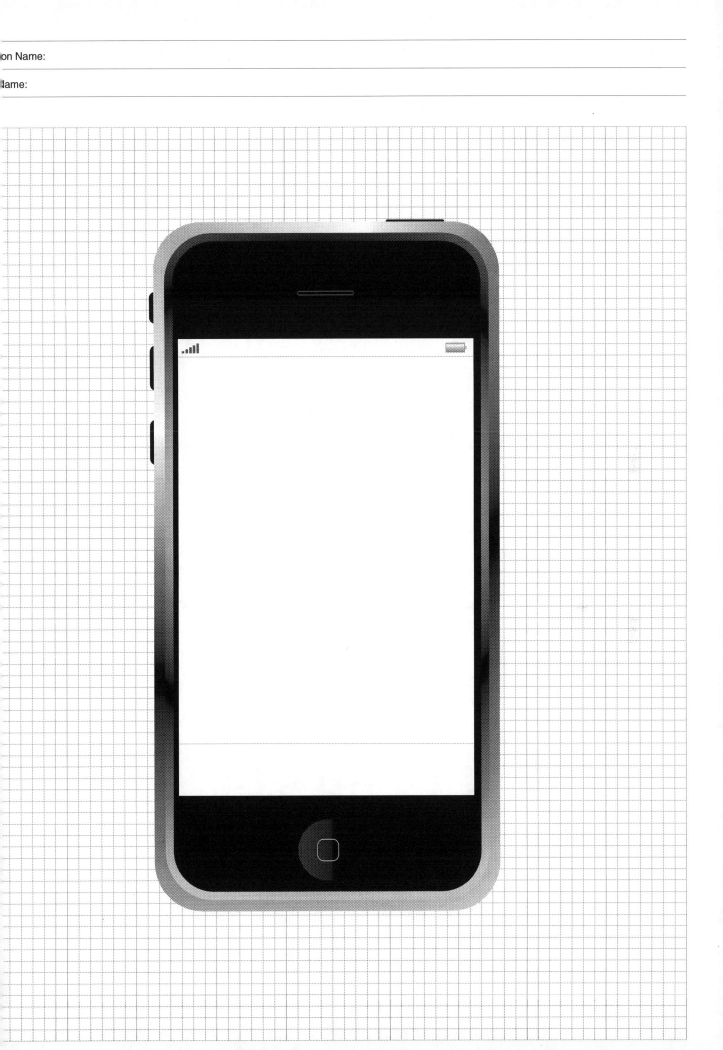

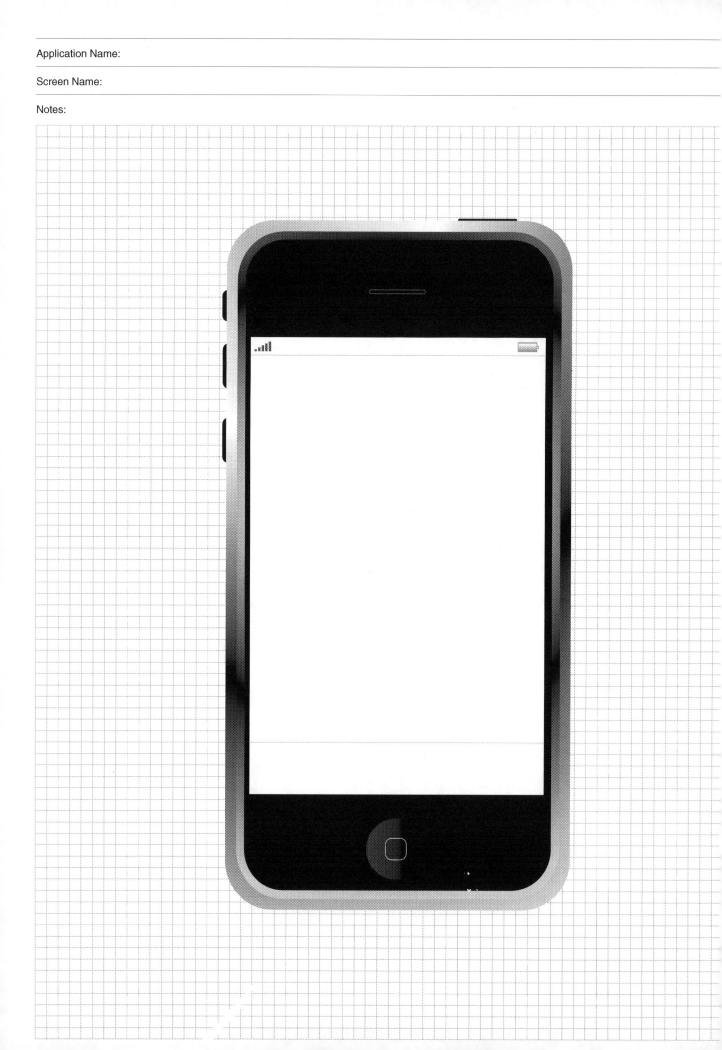

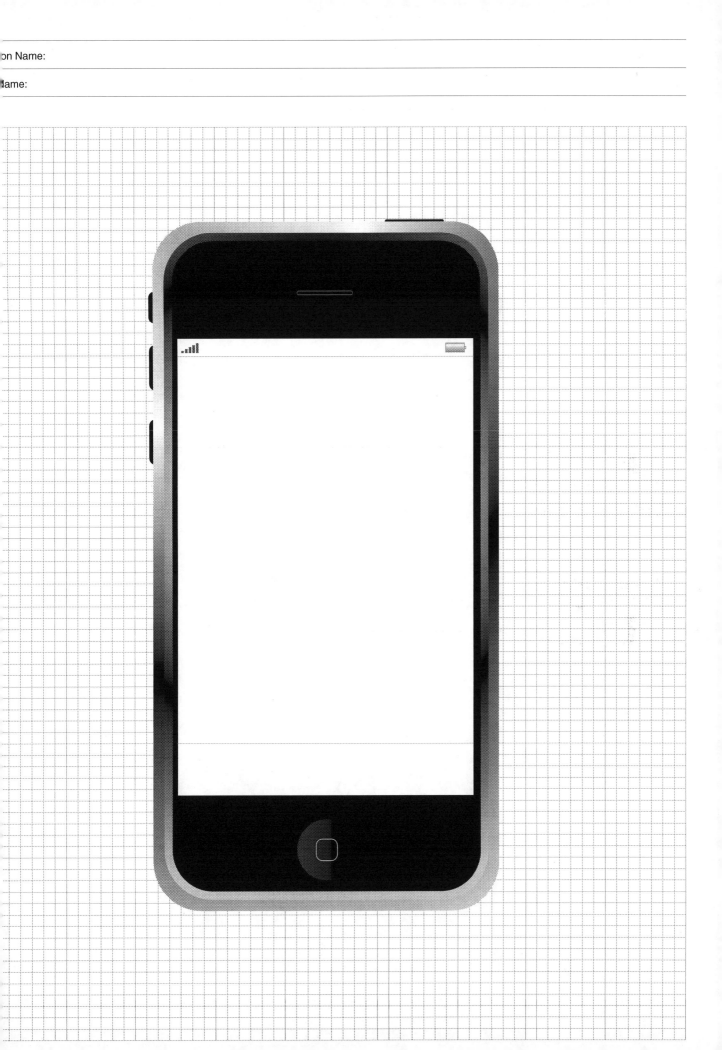

Application Name:

Screen Name:

Notes:

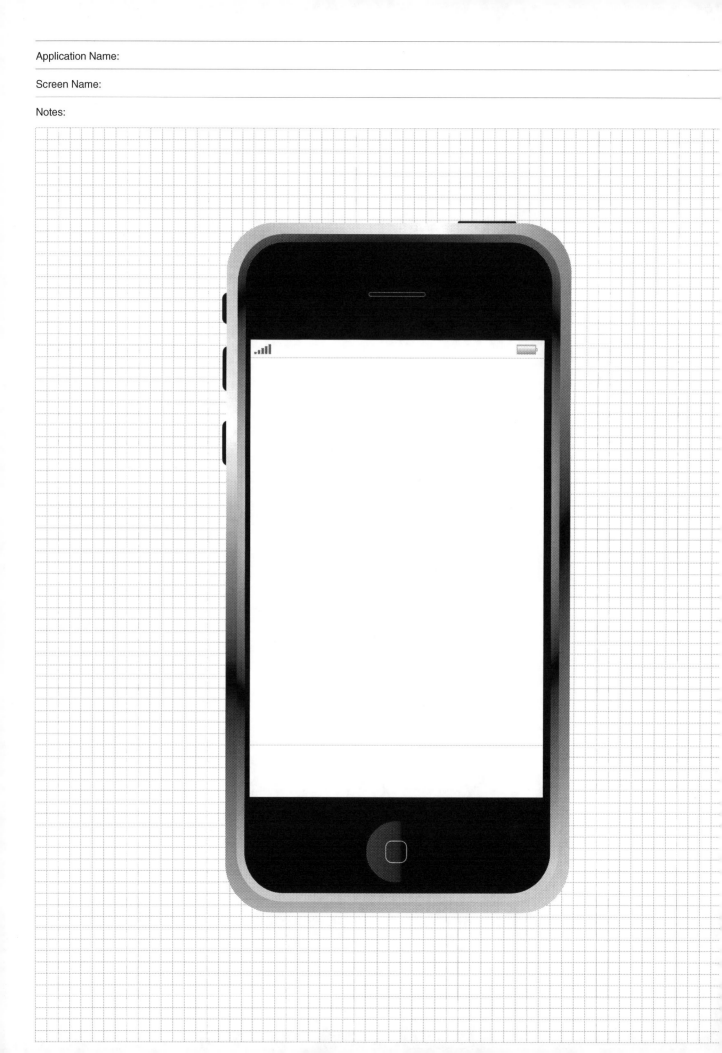

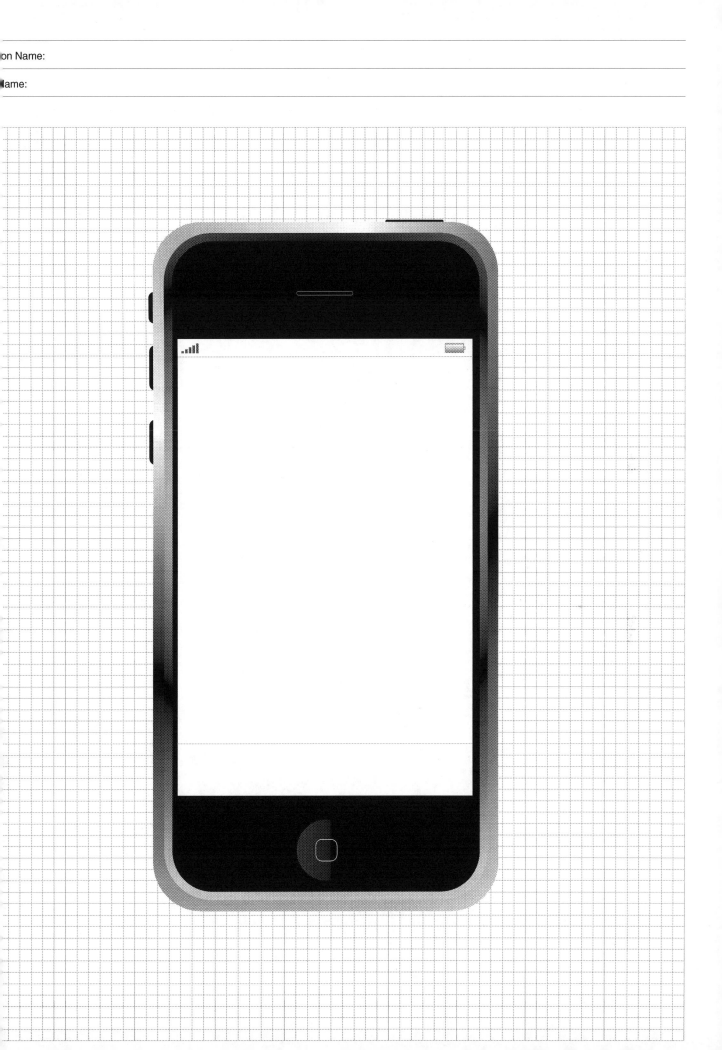

Application Name: _____

Screen Name: _____

Notes:

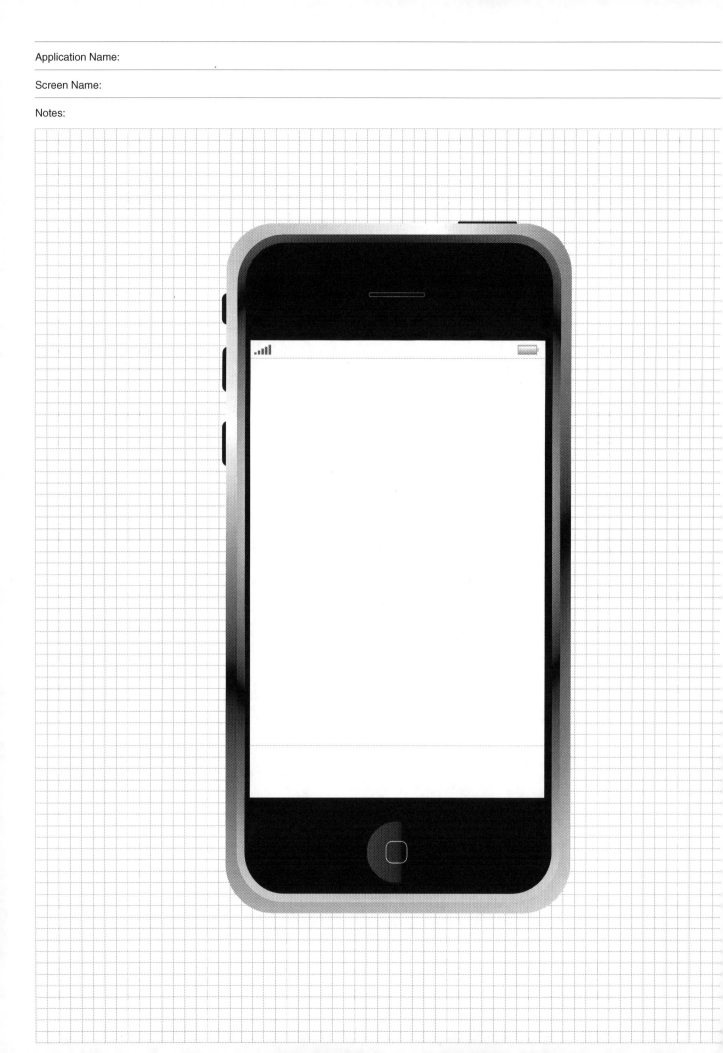

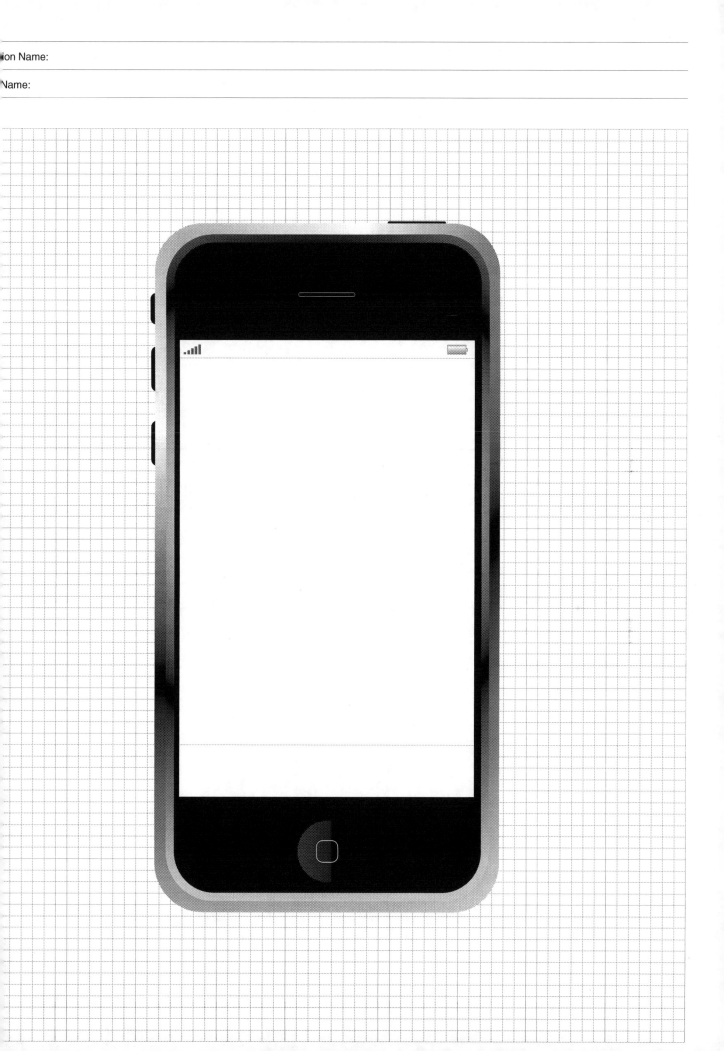

Application Name:

Screen Name:

Notes:

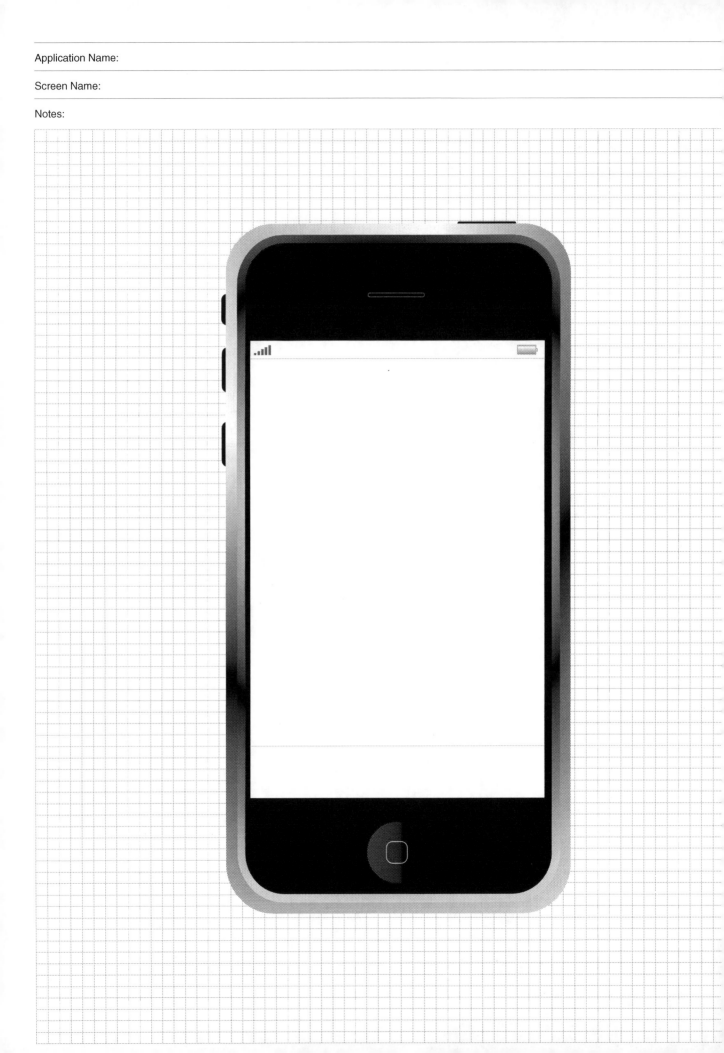

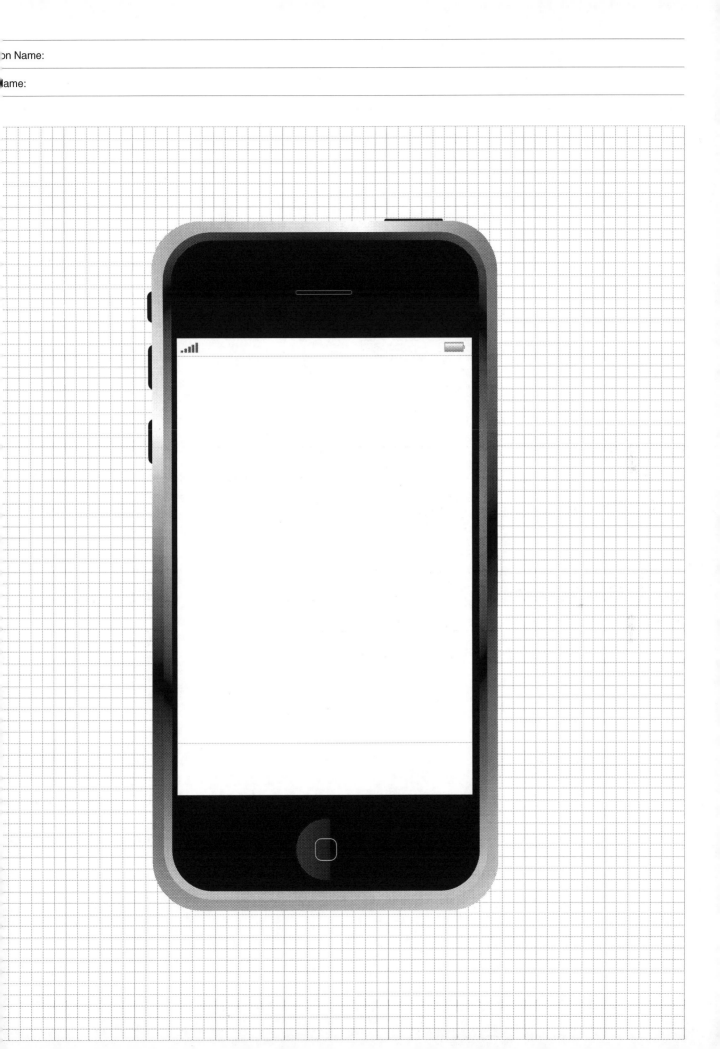

Application Name:

Screen Name:

Notes:

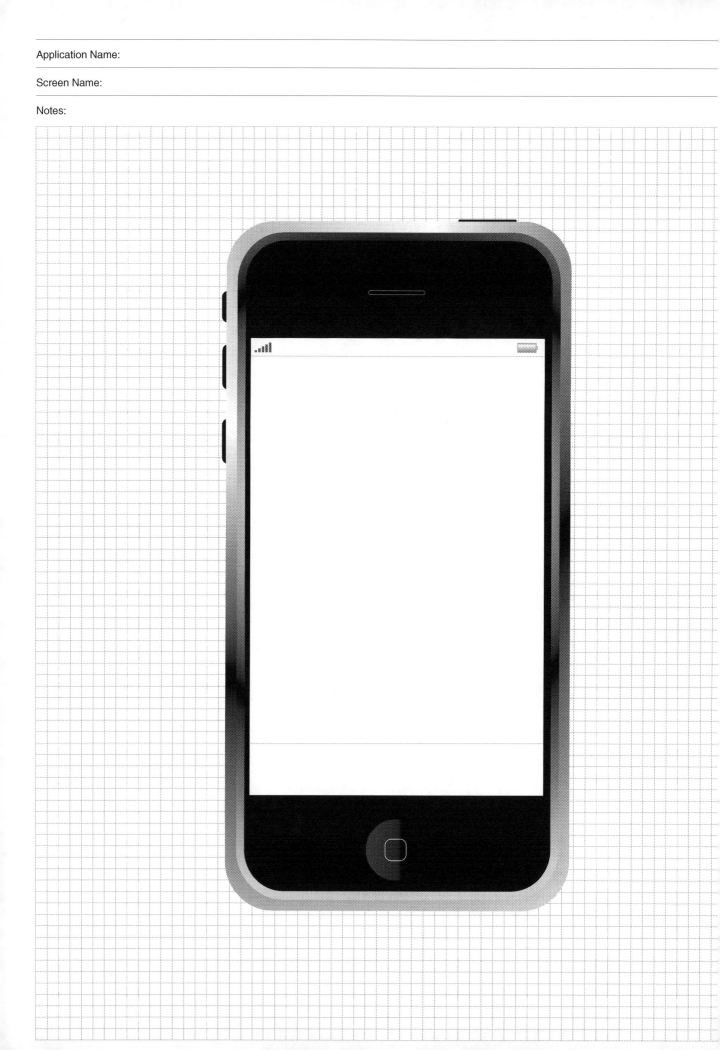

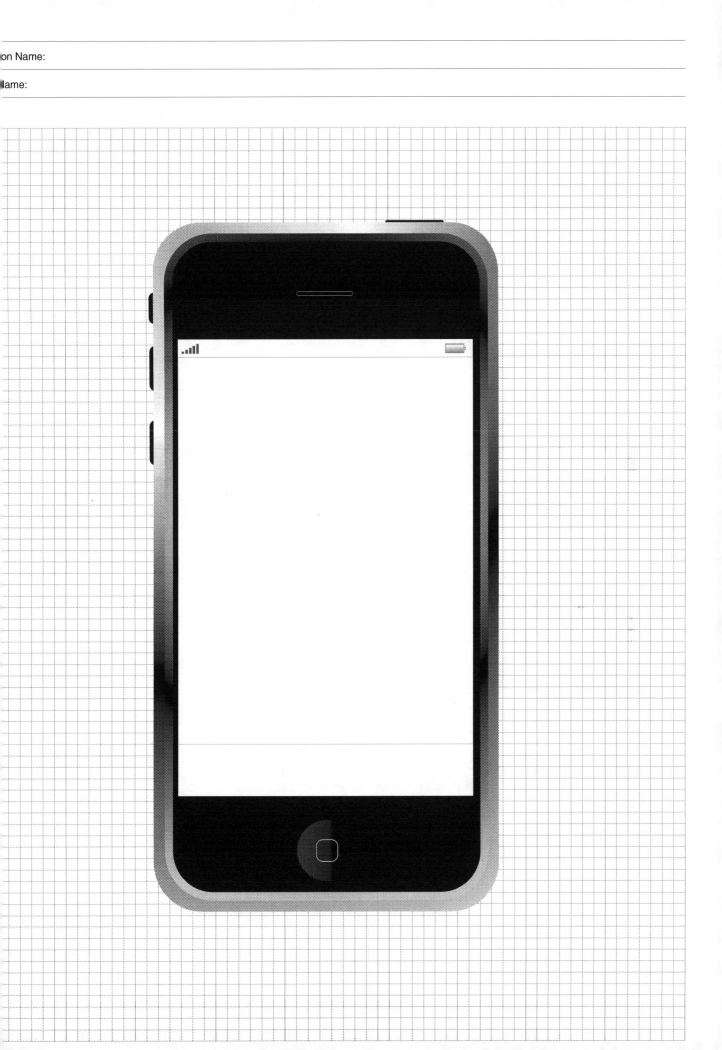

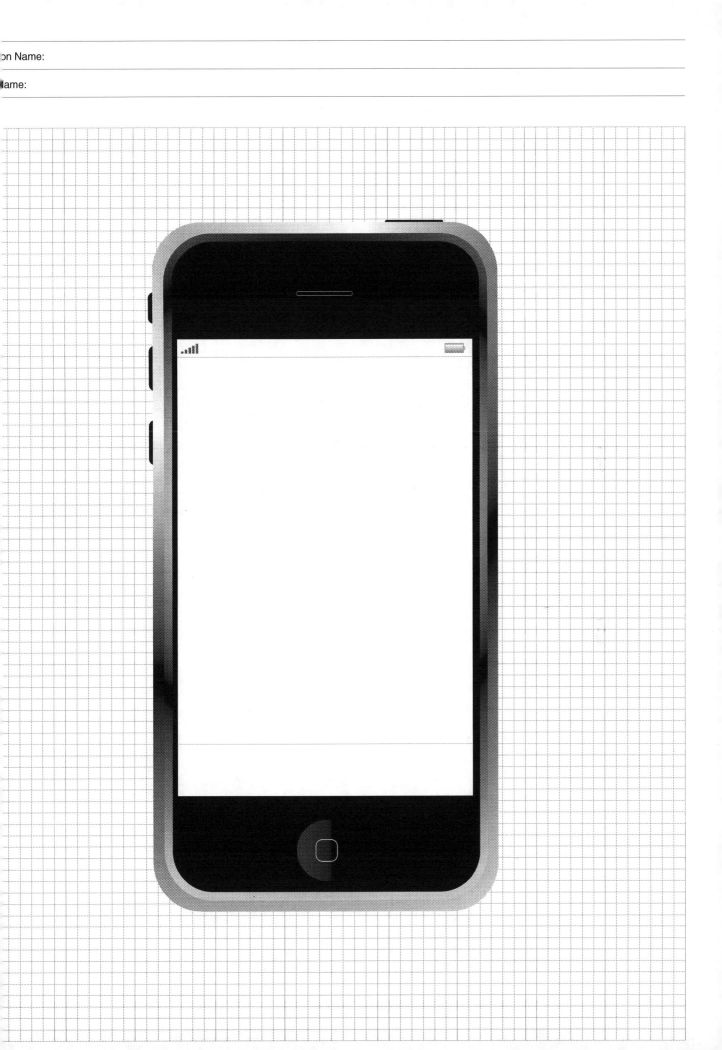

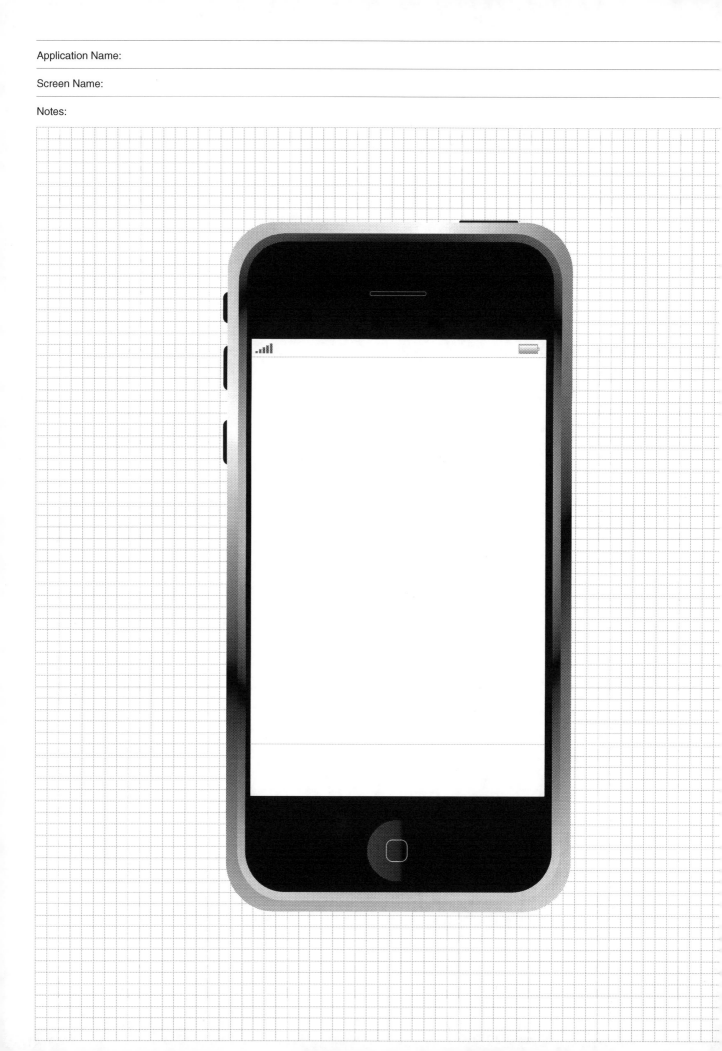

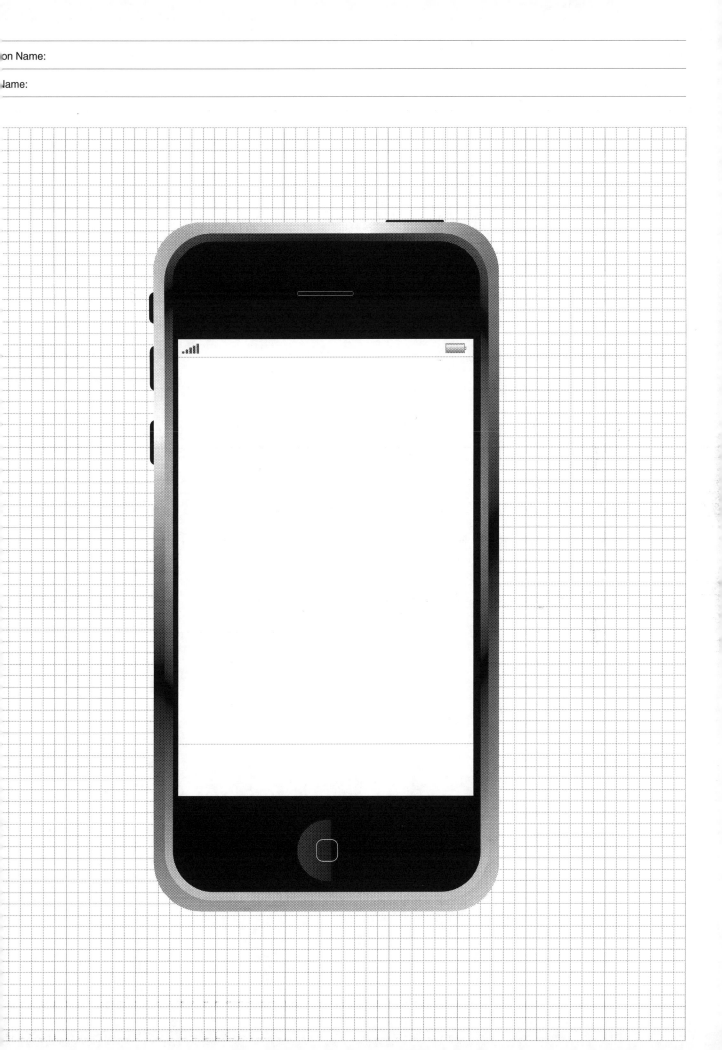

Application Name:

Screen Name:

Notes:

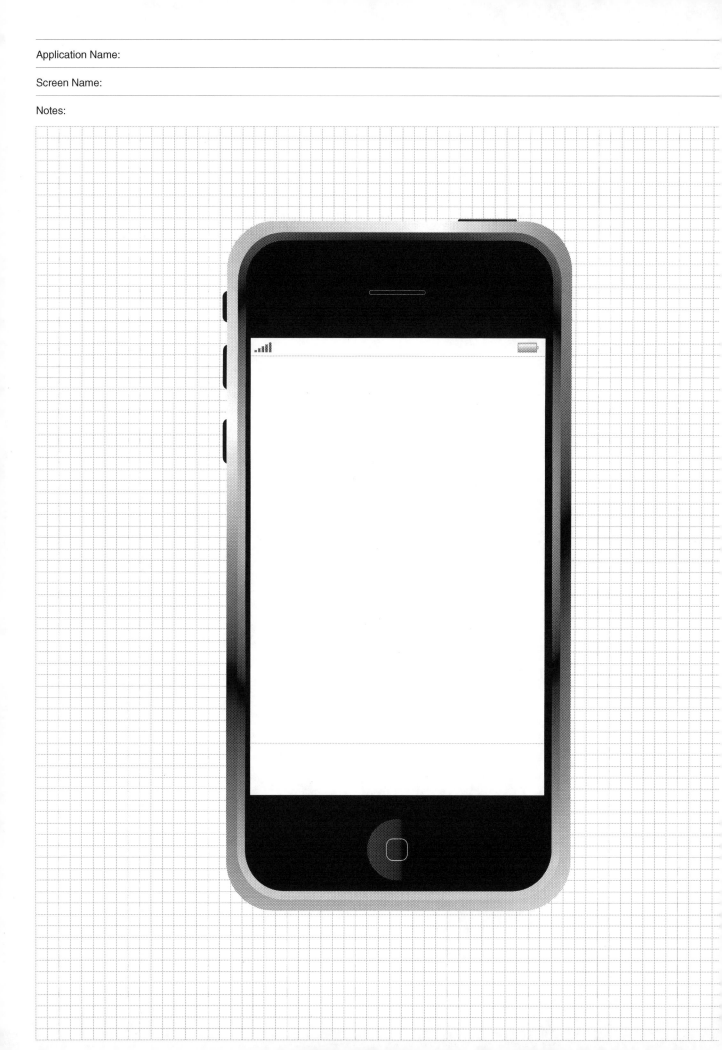

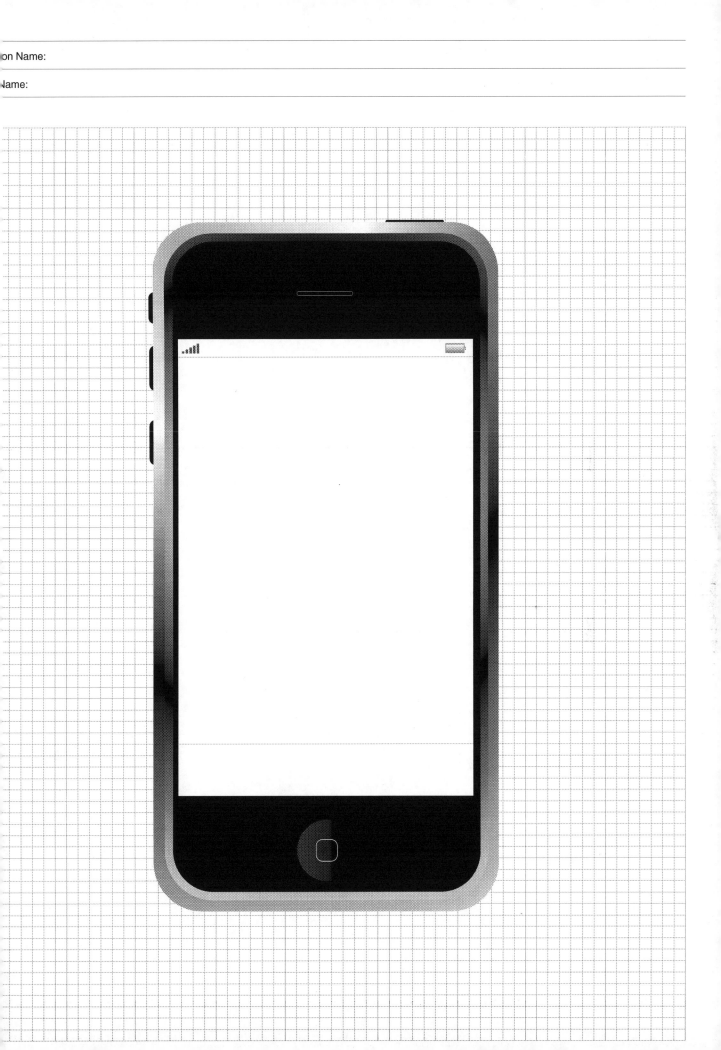

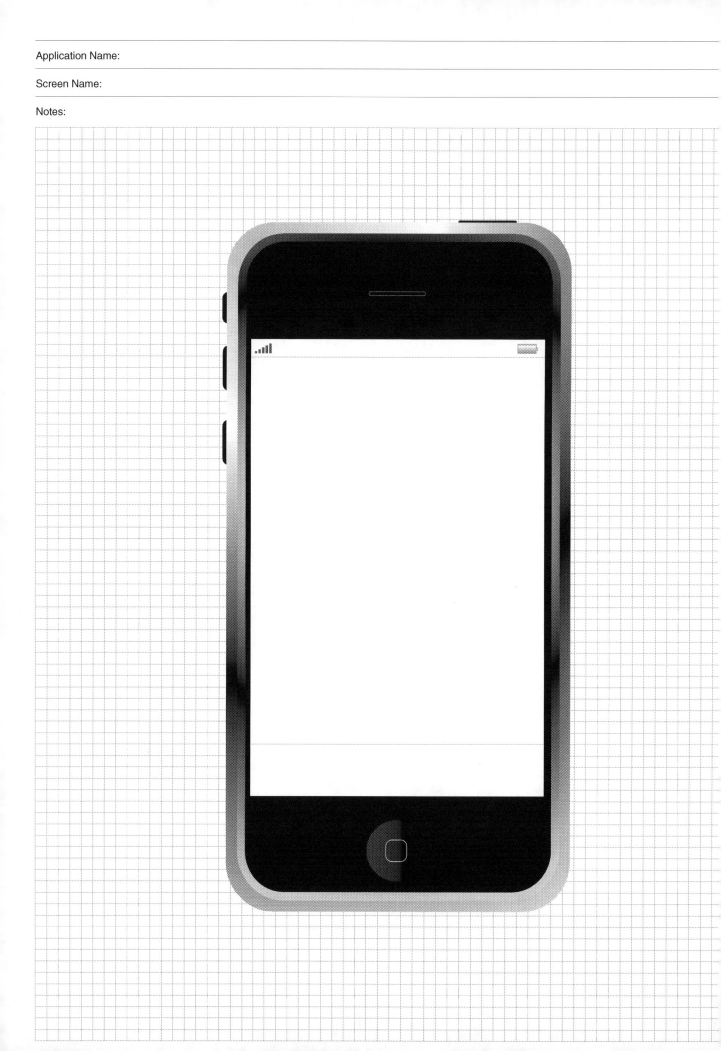

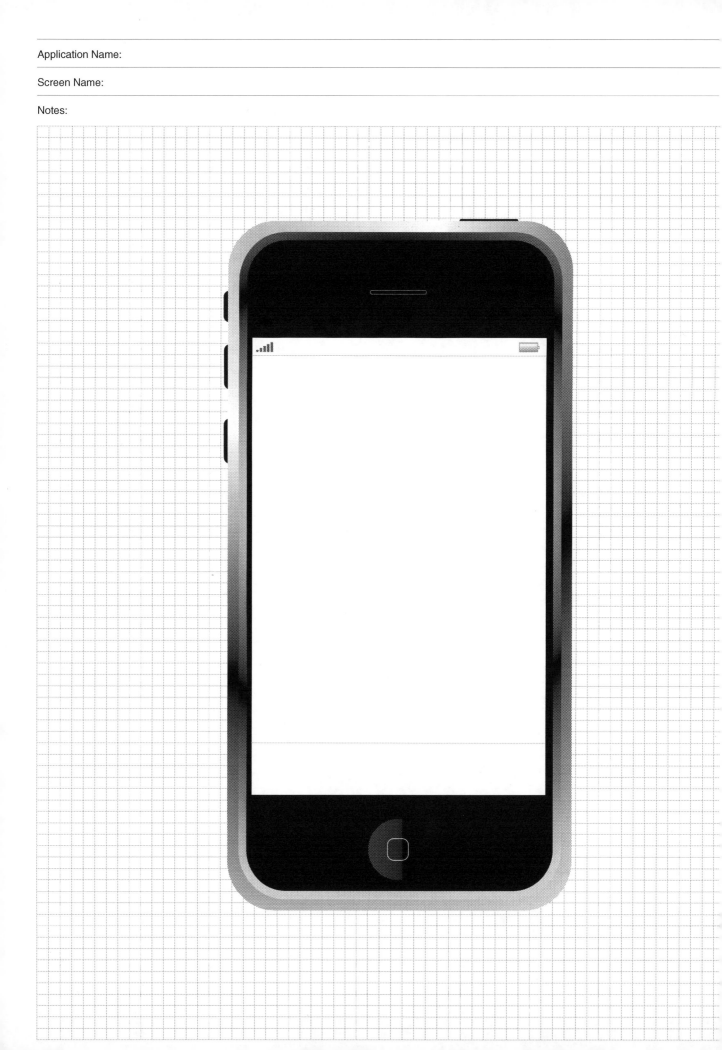

on Name:

Name:

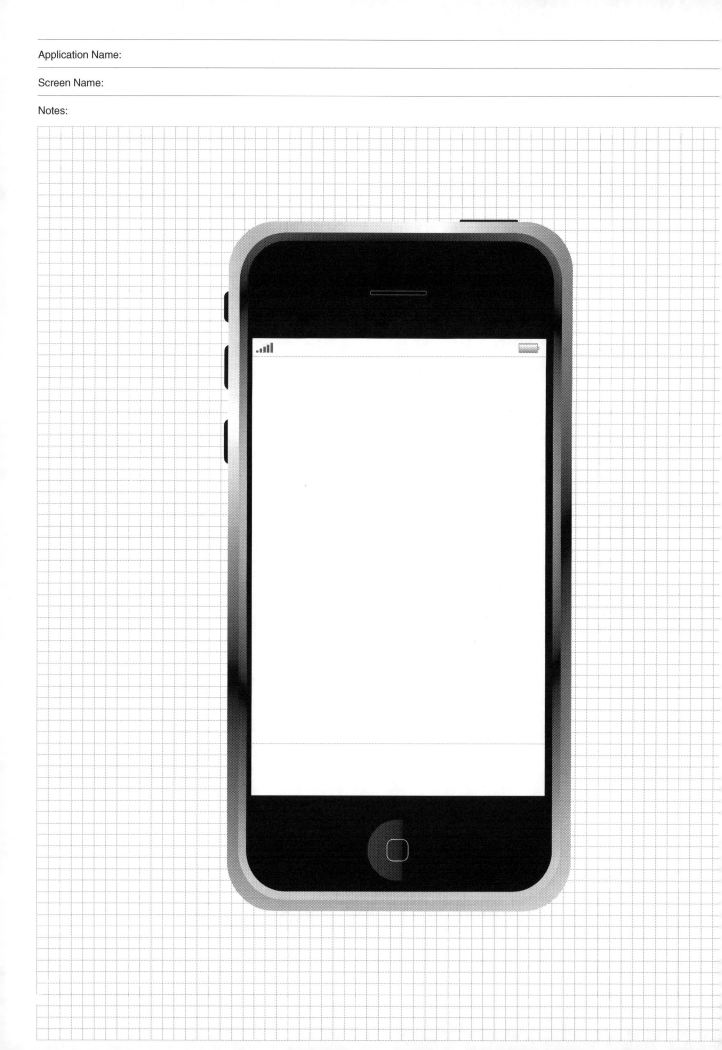

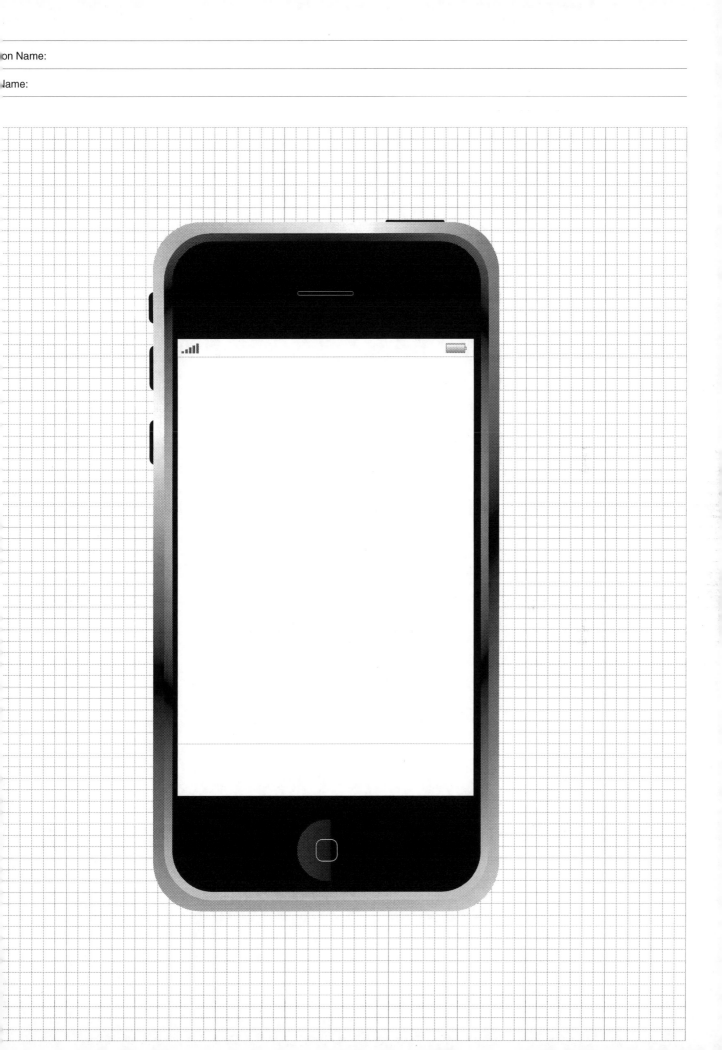

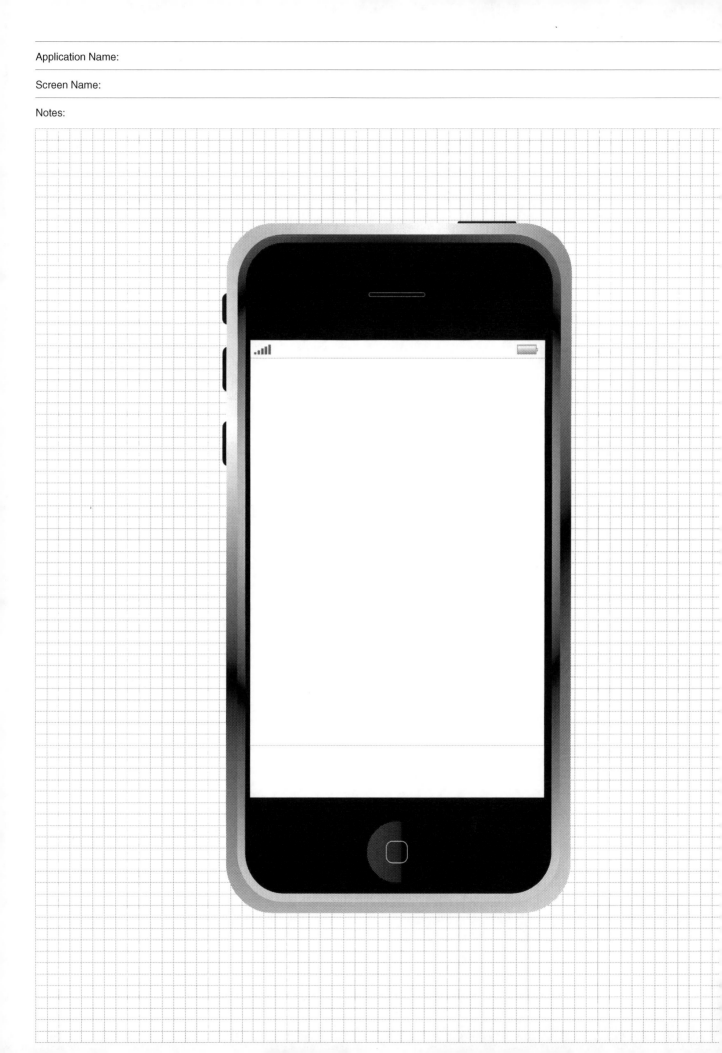

Application Name:

Screen Name:

Notes:

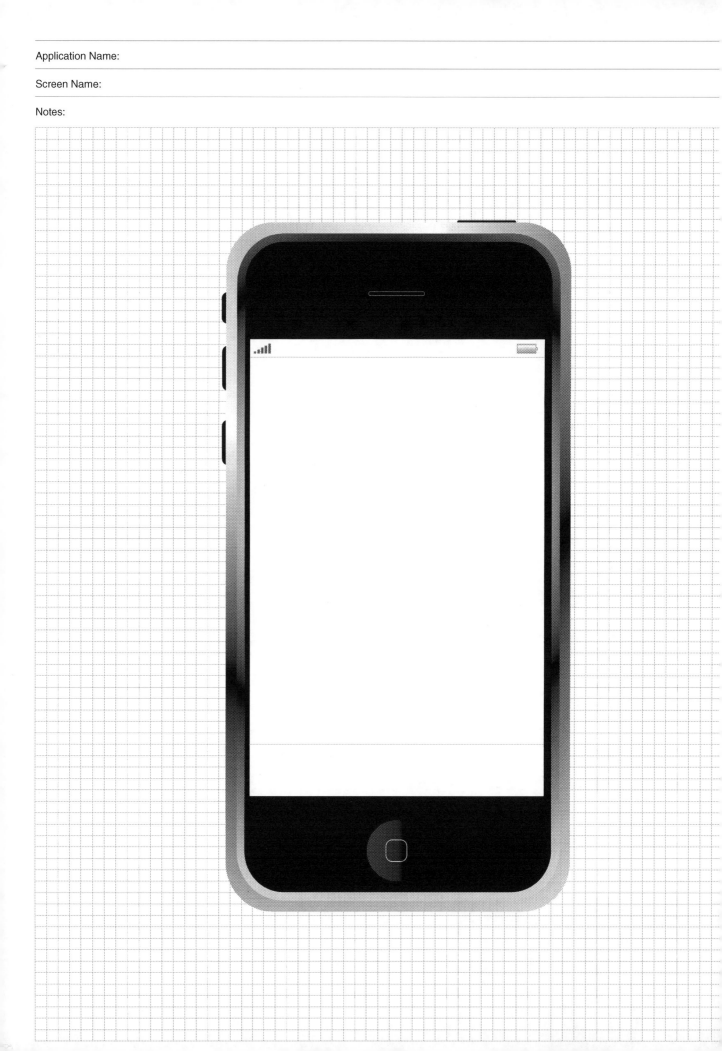

Application Name:

Screen Name:

Notes:

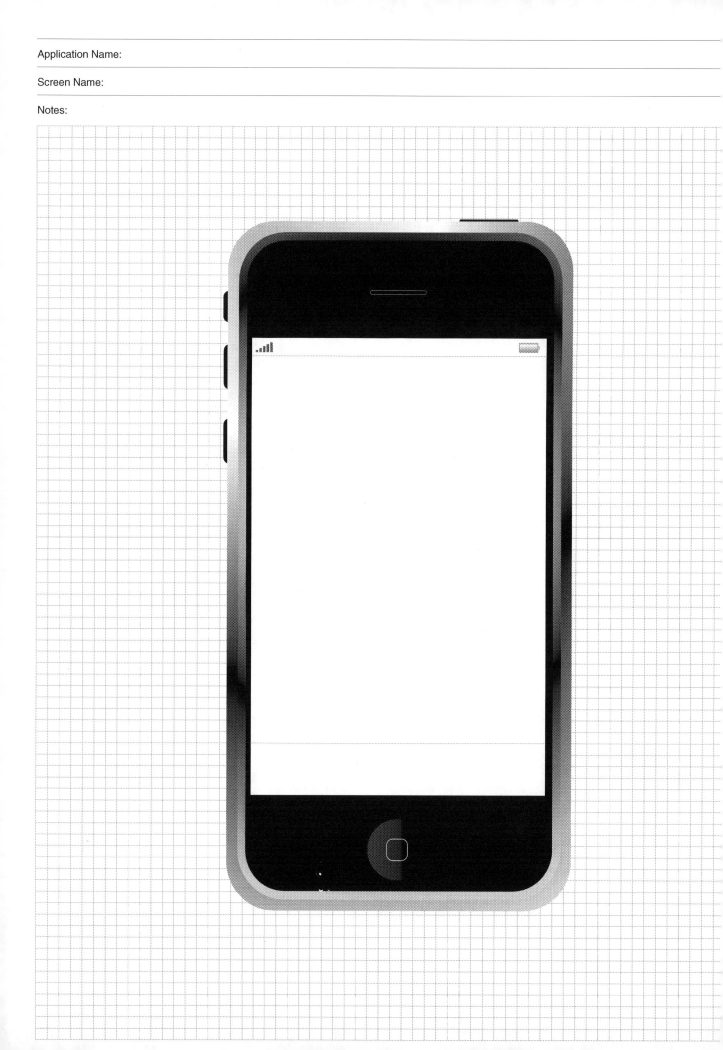

Application Name:

Screen Name:

Notes:

Application Name:

Screen Name:

Notes:

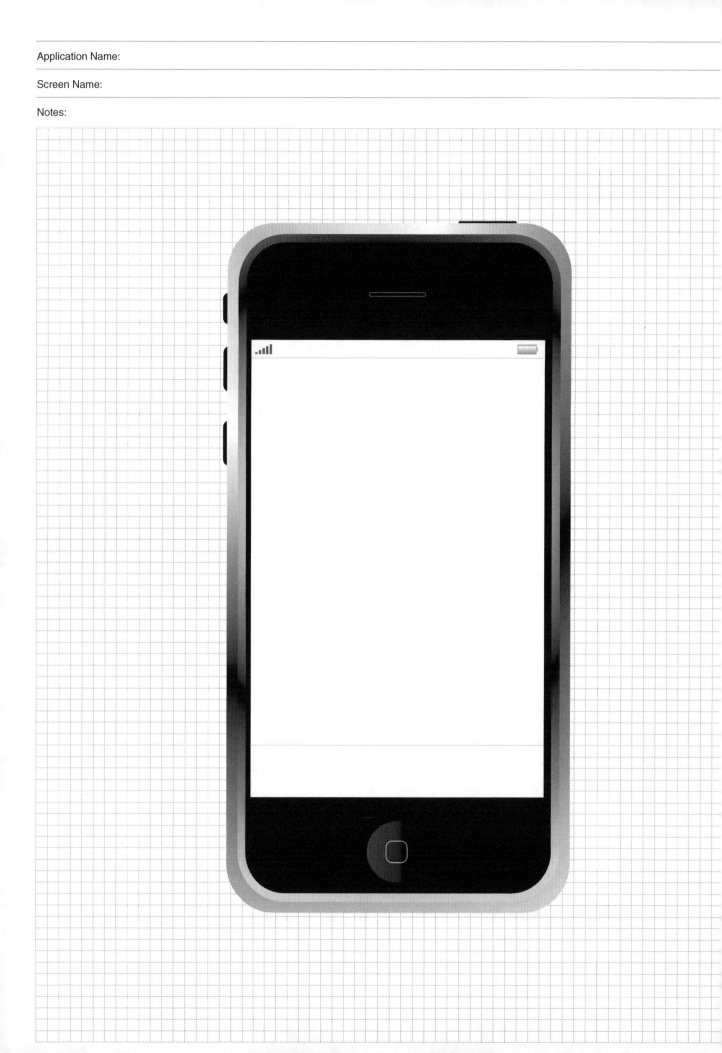

Application Name:

Screen Name:

Notes:

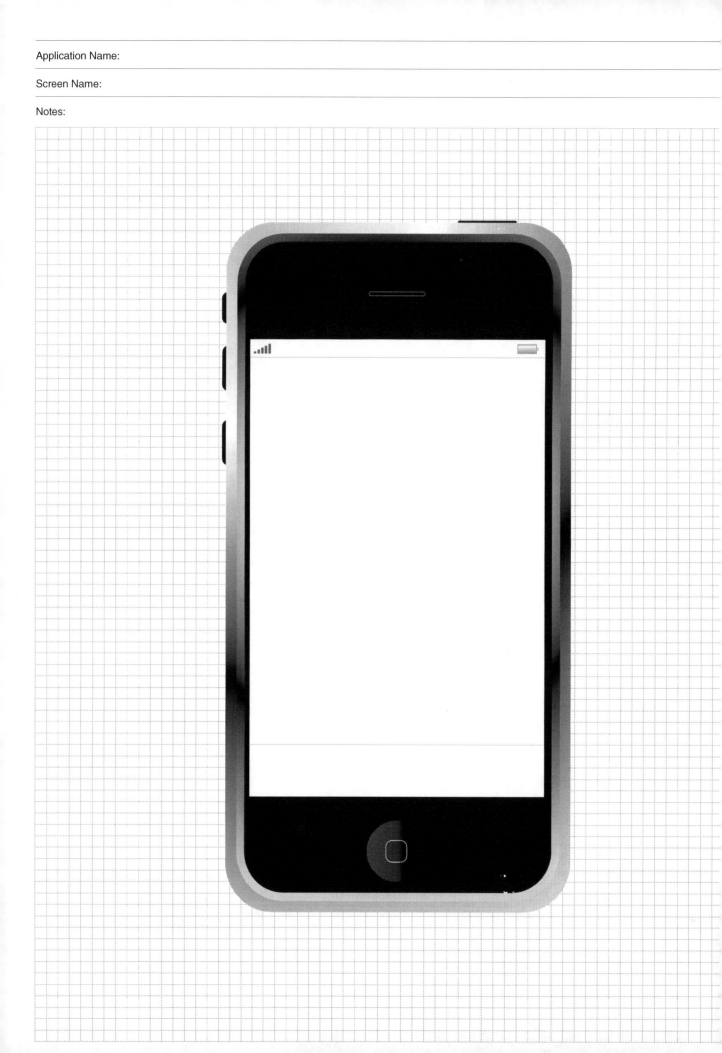

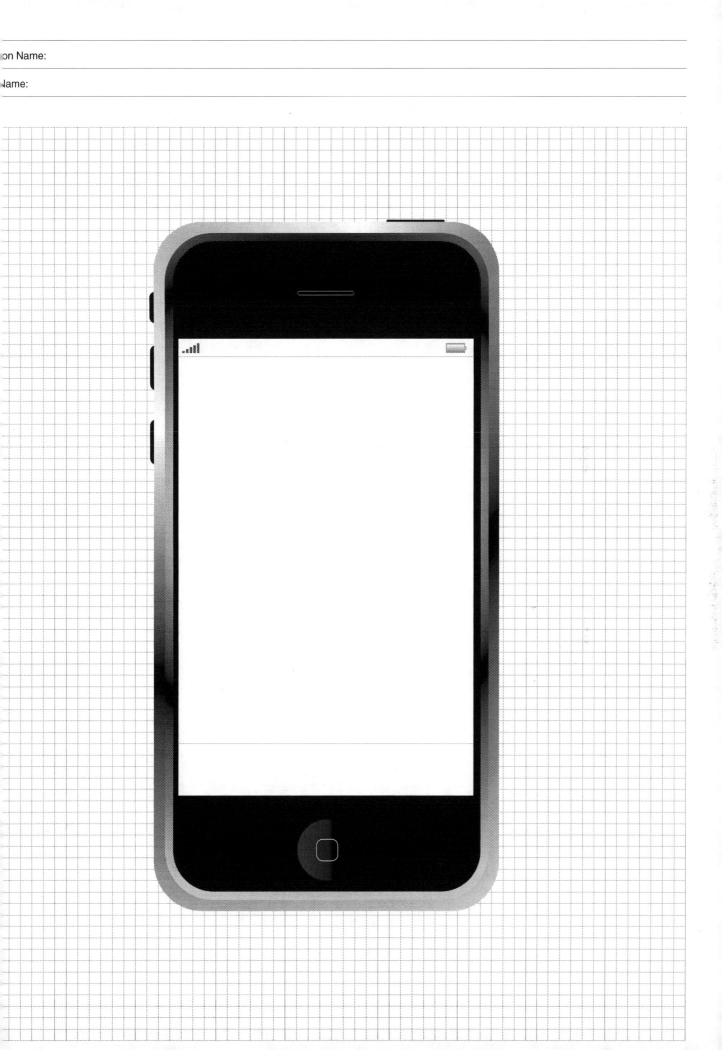

Application Name:

Screen Name:

Notes:

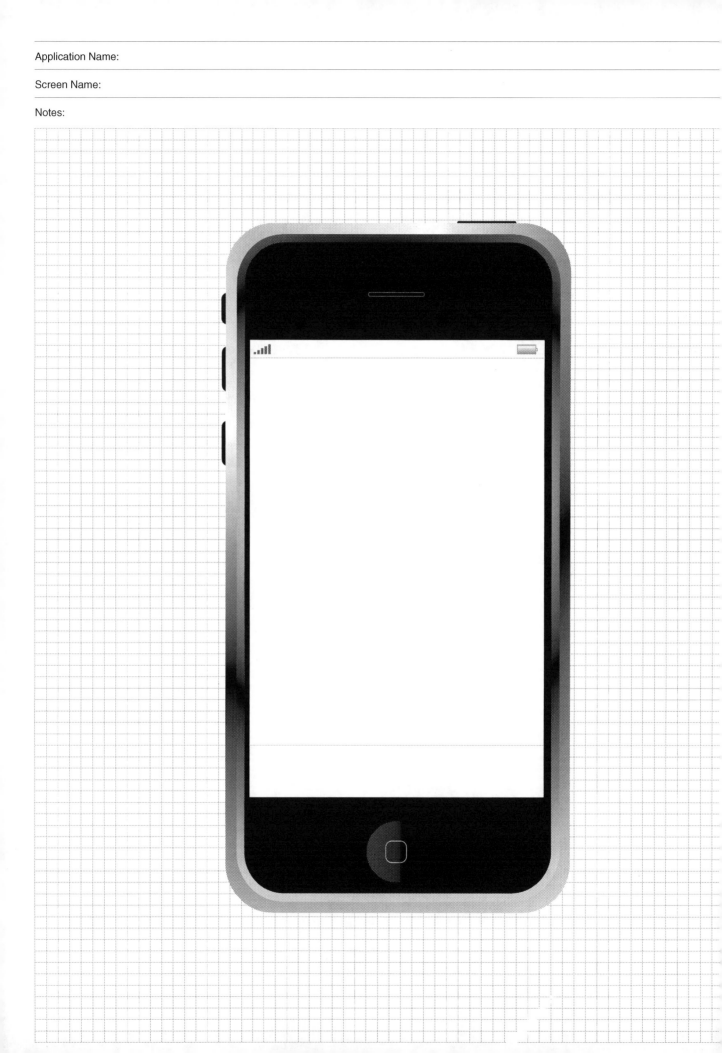

Application Name:

Screen Name:

Notes:

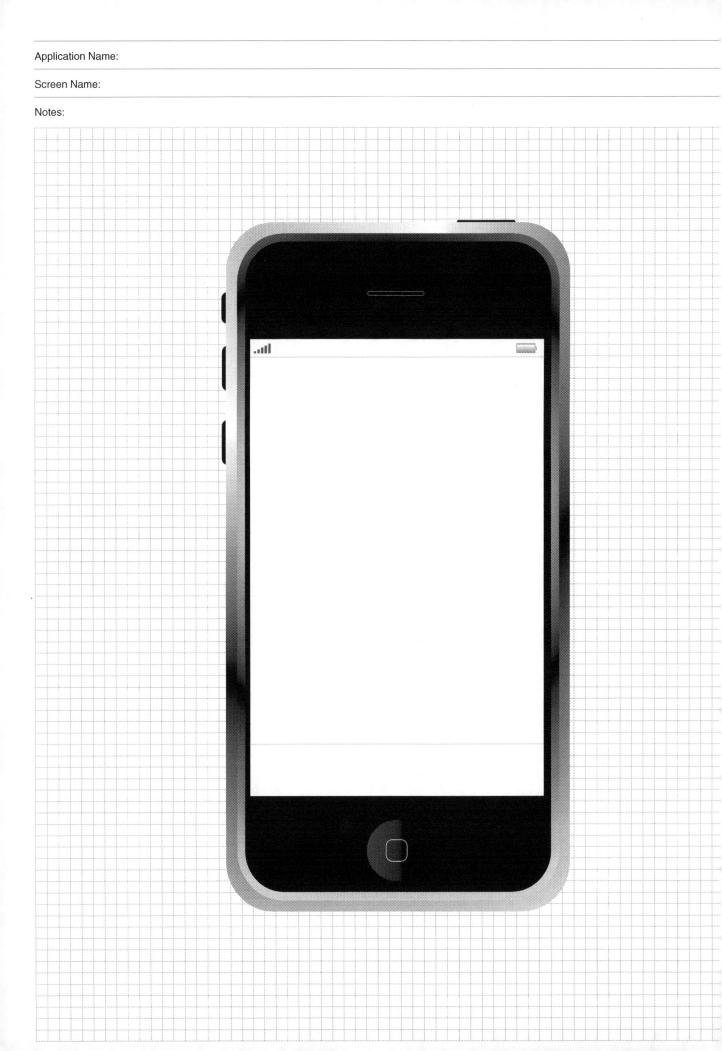

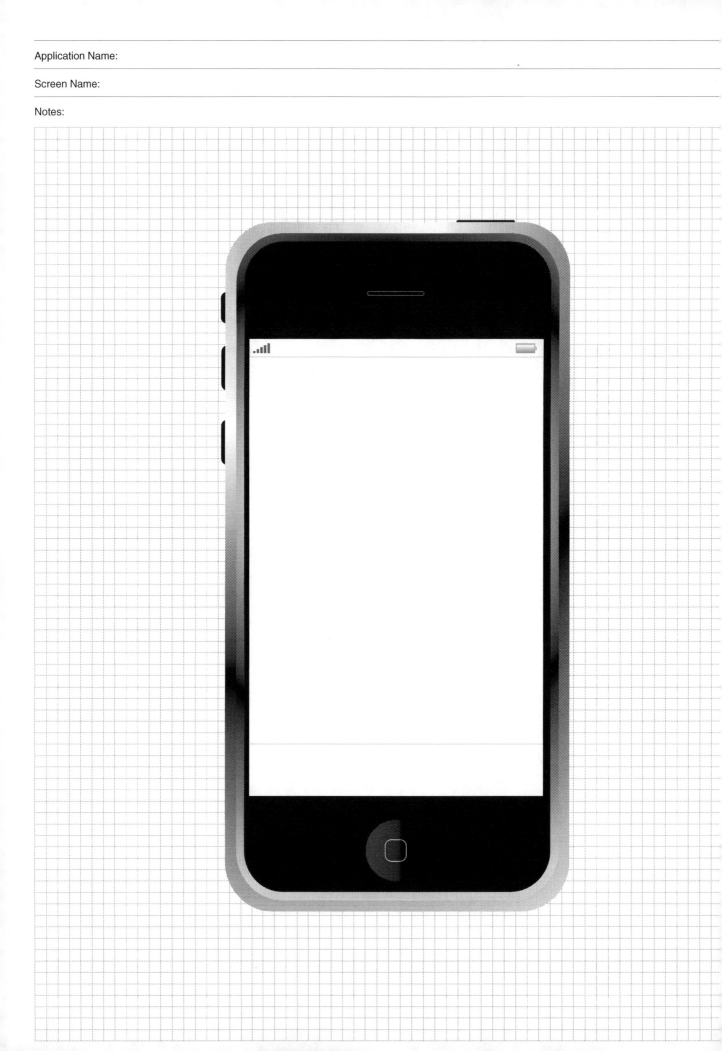

on Name:

Name:

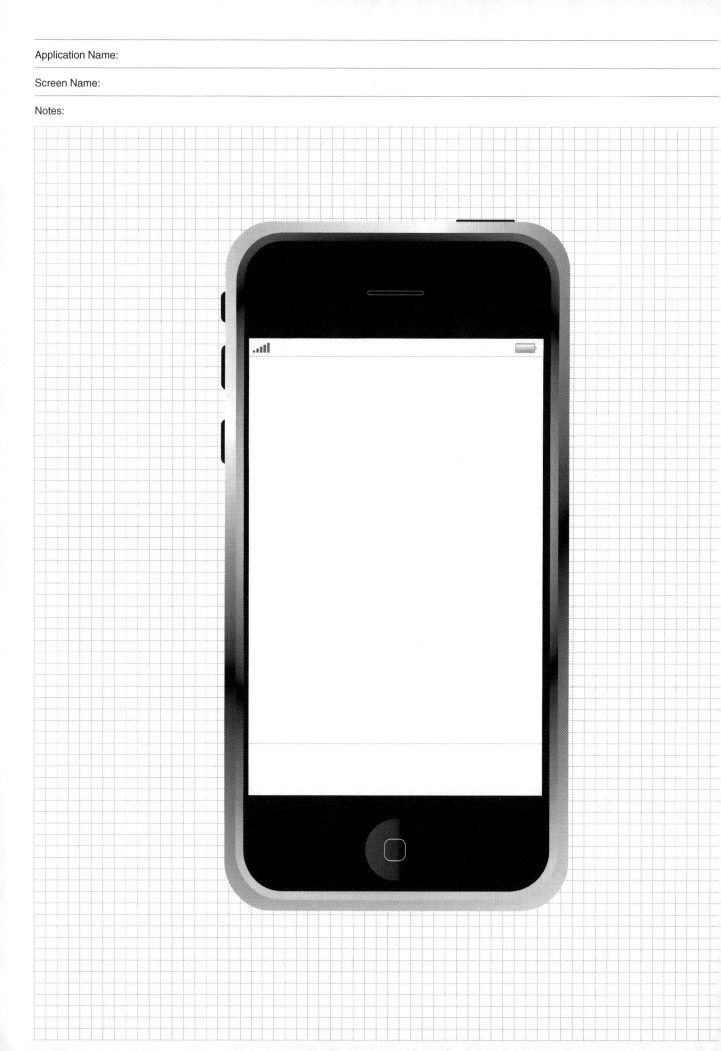

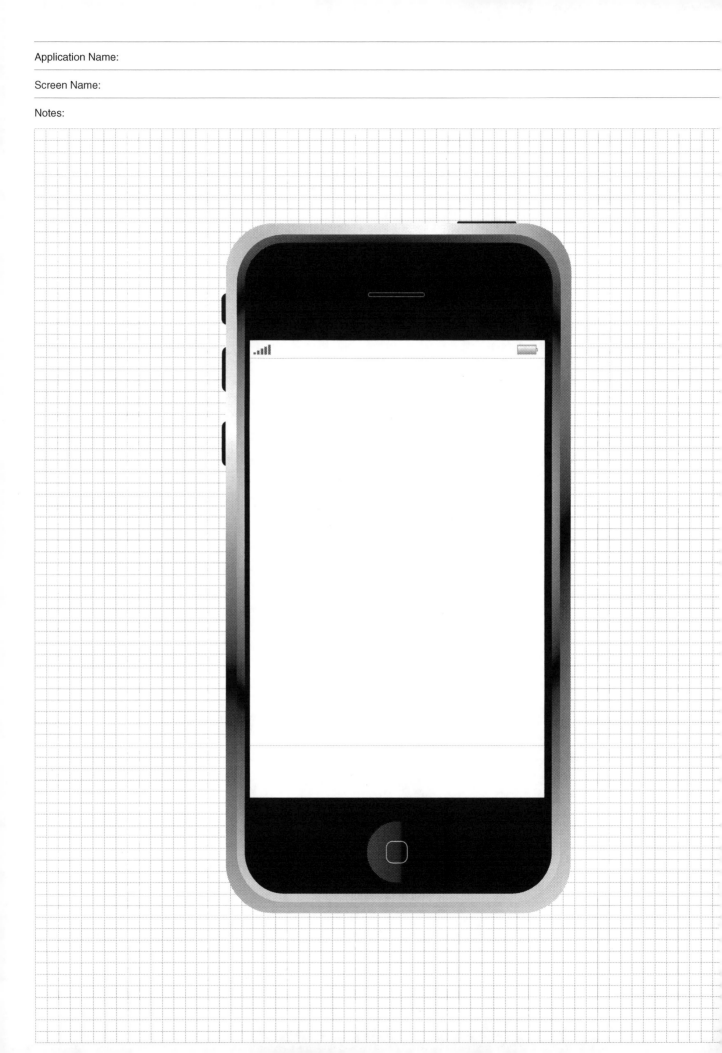

Application Name:

Screen Name:

Notes:

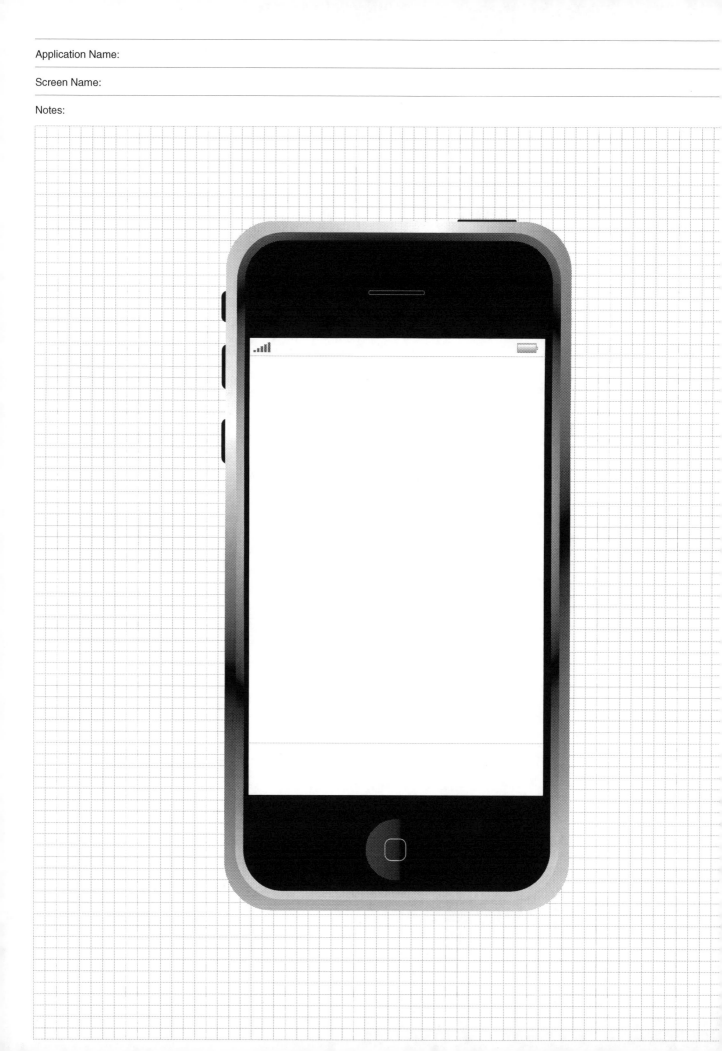